Dear valued reader,

Thank you for purchasing "How to Draw Cats by Grid". We hope that this book will provide you with hours of creative enjoyment and help you to develop your drawing skills.

To use this book, simply choose a cat image from the book and study it carefully. Then, using the blank grid provided below, recreate the image by drawing each section of the cat within the corresponding box on the grid.

The grid system is designed to help you with the proportions of each element in the cat's image, and to help you get a better sense of the overall structure.

However, it's important to remember that this book is just a guide, and you are encouraged to experiment and use your own unique art style. You don't have to create an exact replica of the cat image, have fun and let your creativity flow!

Throughout the book, you will also find interesting cat facts on every other page, which we hope you will enjoy as you progress through your drawing journey.

Thank you again for choosing "How to Draw Cats by Grid", and we wish you all the best in your artistic endeavors.

Sincerely,

L J Harris

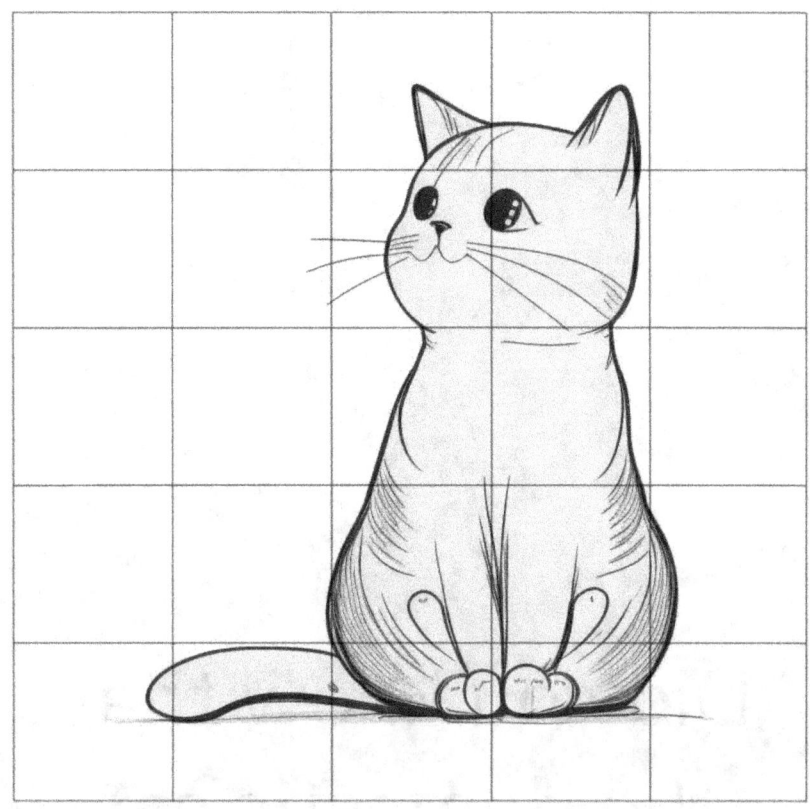

Did you know that
the domestic cat
descends from the
African Wildcat?

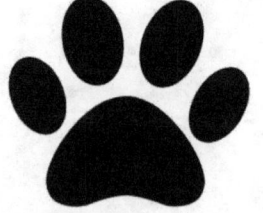

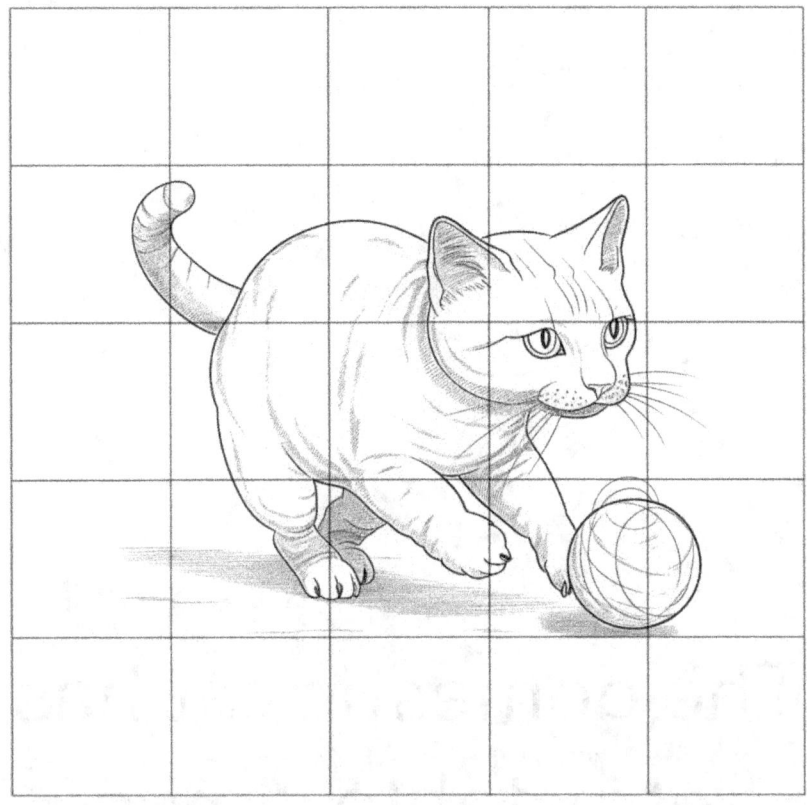

The domestic cat has
retractable claws,
this is used to climb
and hunt.

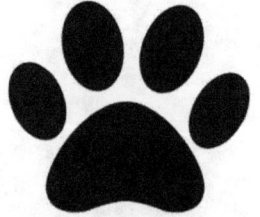

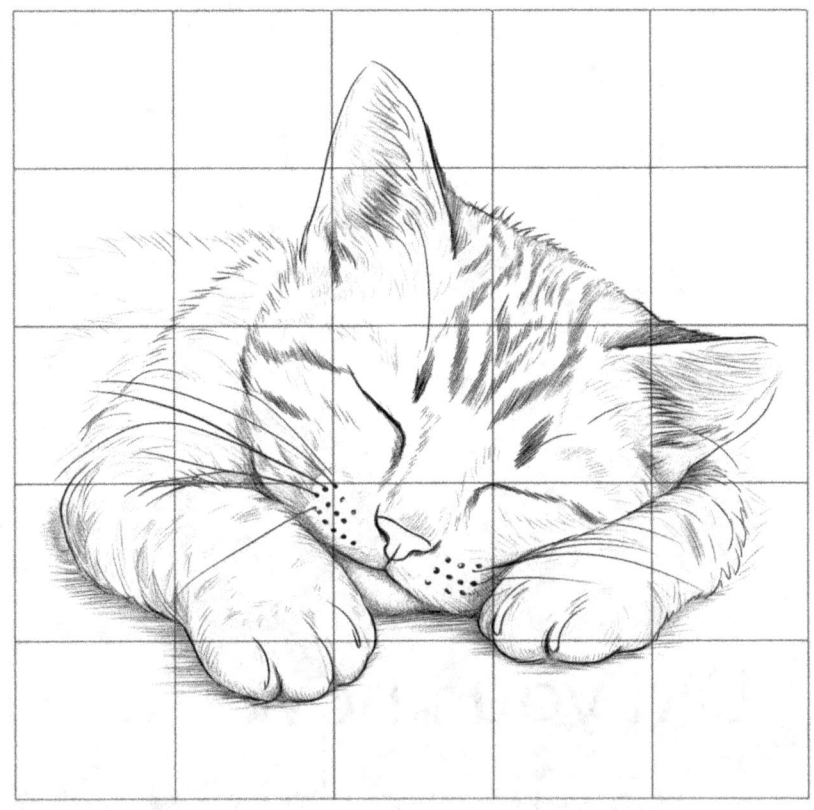

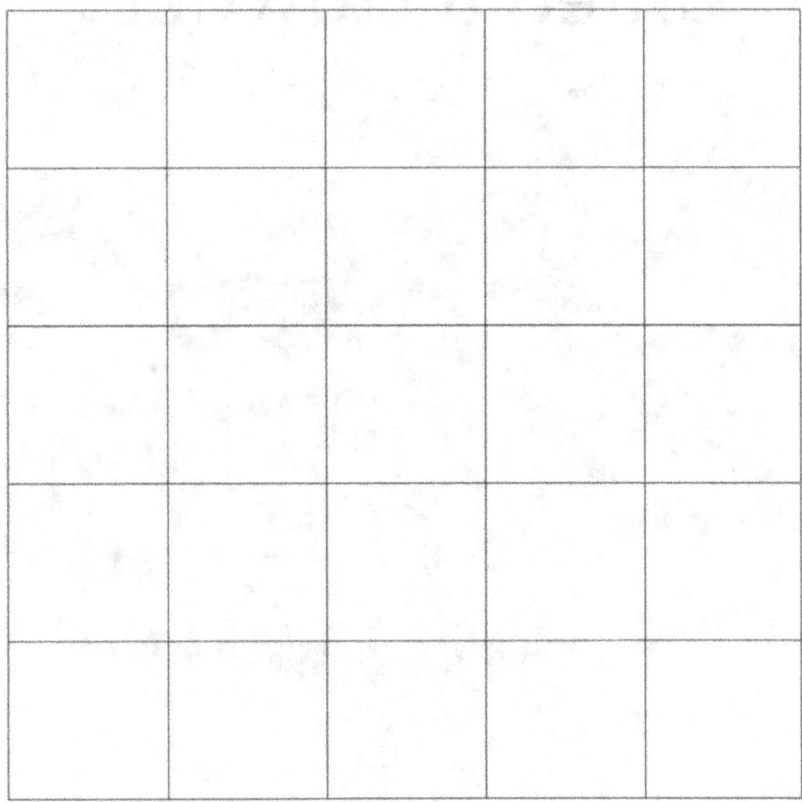

Did you know that
group of cats is
called a clowder?

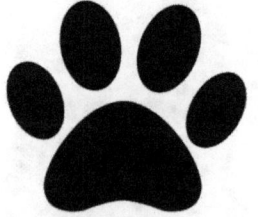

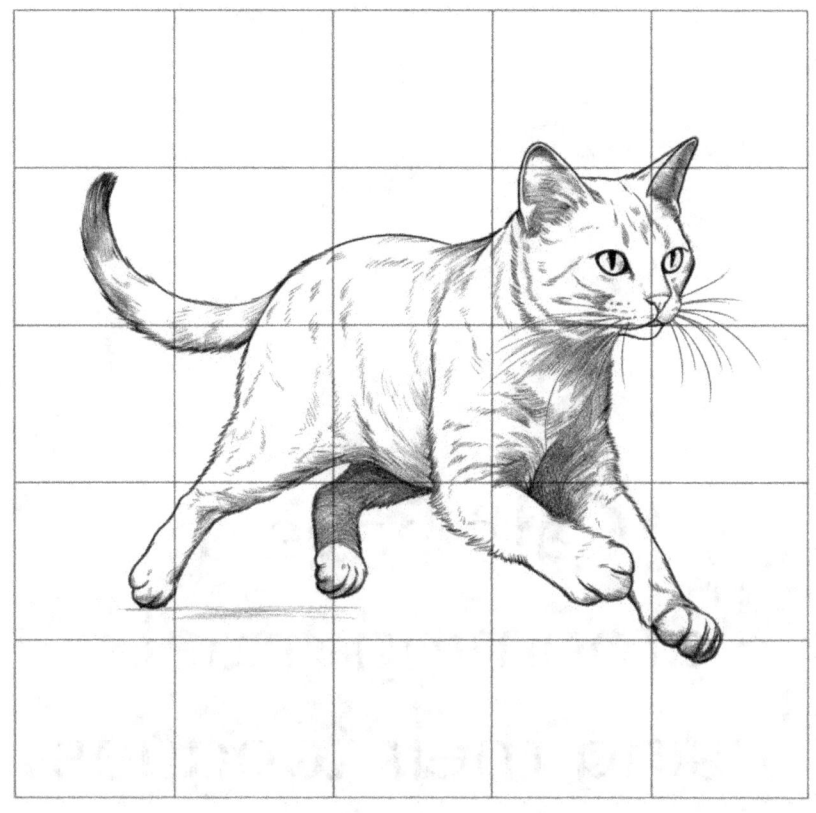

Cats have a
grooming ritual,
using their tongues
to clean themselves
and distribute
natural oils to keep
their fur healthy.

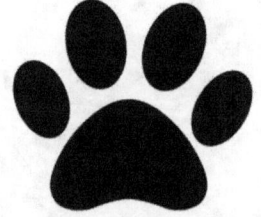

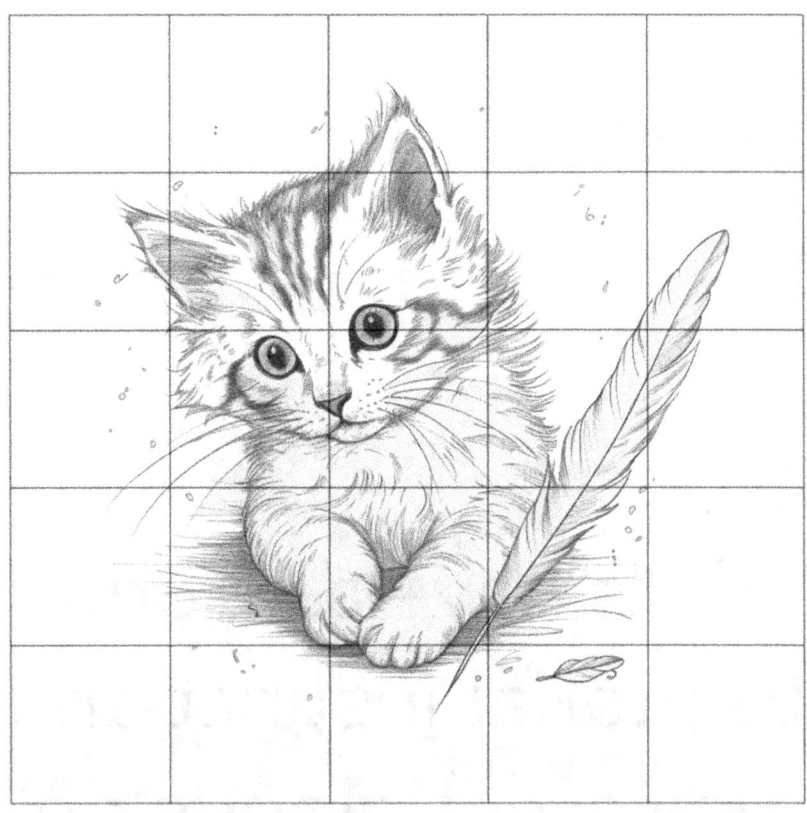

Cats have a strong
territorial instinct and
use scent glands on
their cheeks, paws,
and tail base to mark
their territory.

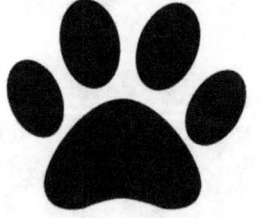

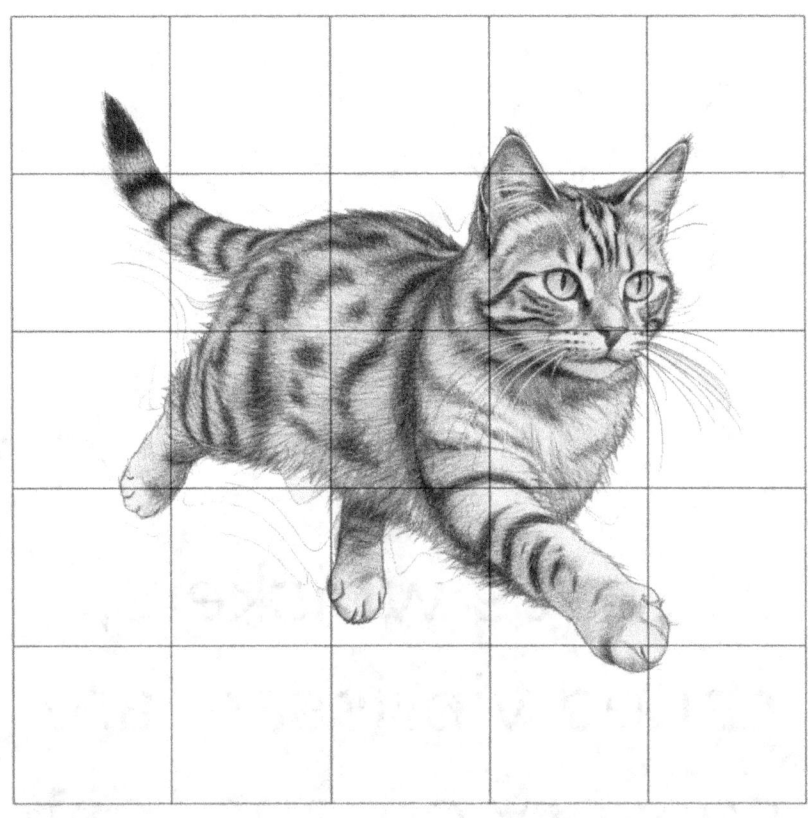

A cat's whiskers,
called vibrissae, are
sensory organs that
help them navigate
their environment.

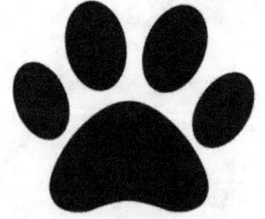

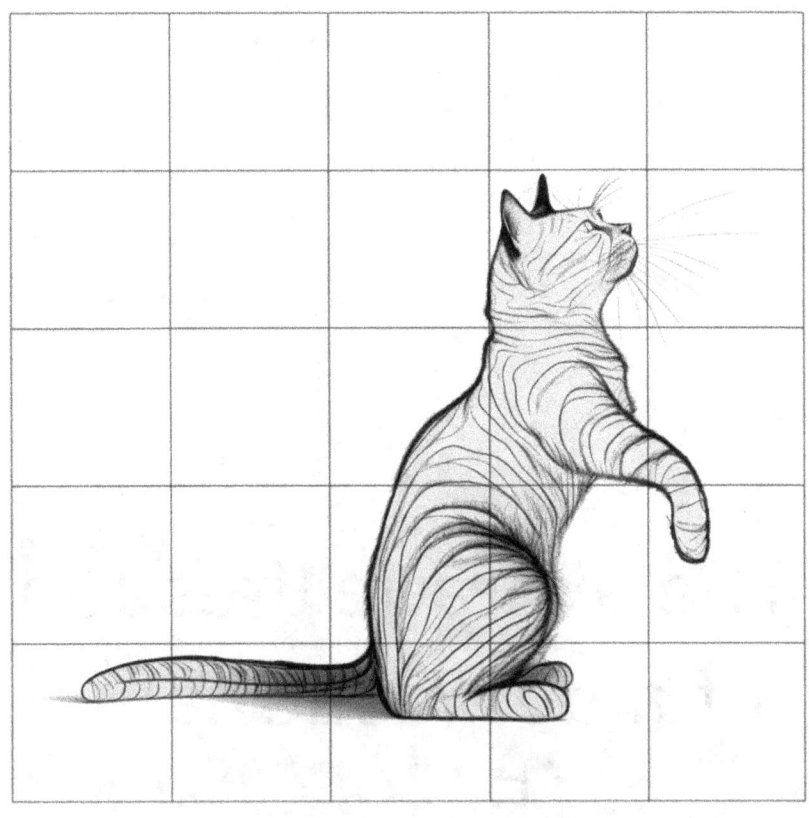

The average lifespan
of a domestic cat is
12-15 years, but
some cats can live
into their 20s.

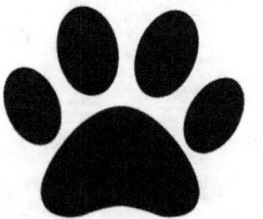

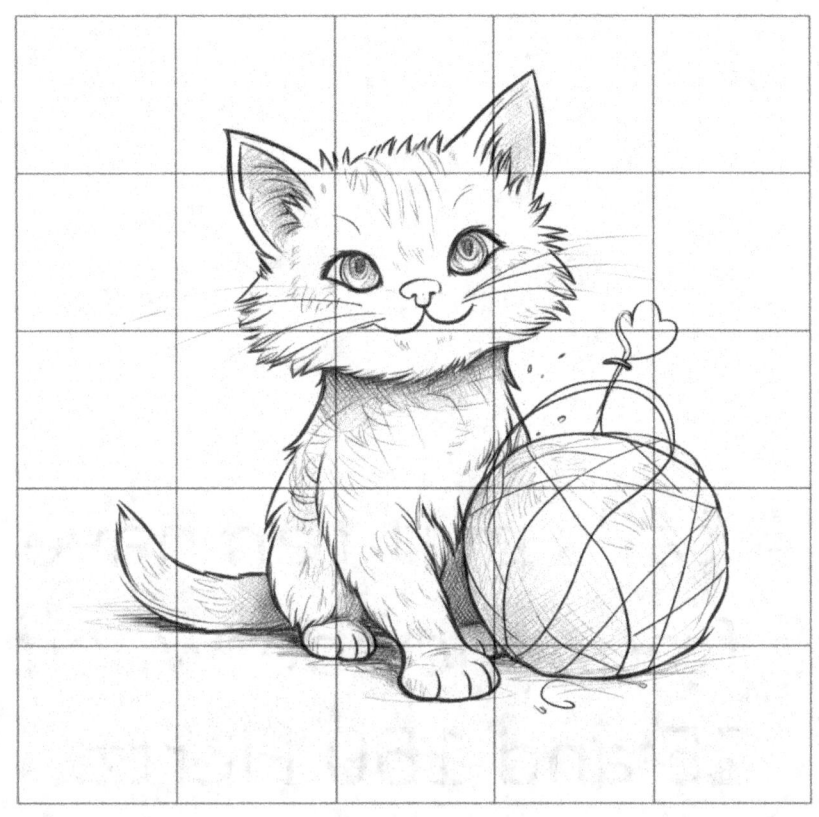

A cat's purr can have a frequency between 25 and 150 Hertz, which is thought to promote healing and relaxation in both cats and humans.

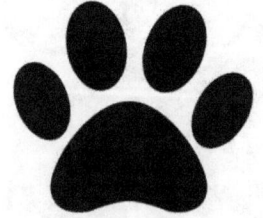

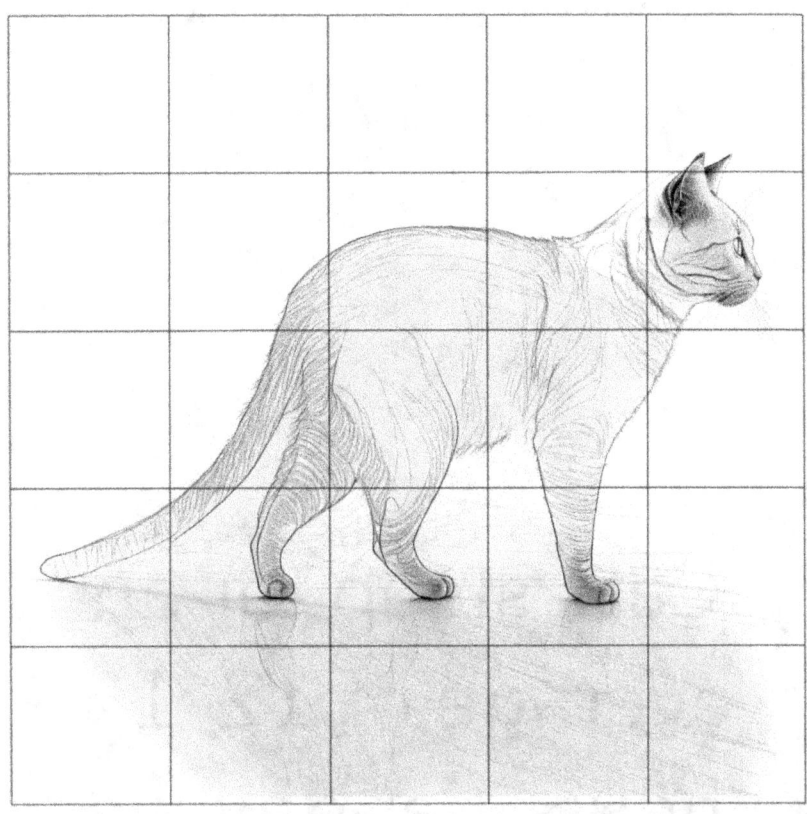

Cats sleep for an average of 12-16 hours per day, as their ancestors needed to conserve energy for hunting.

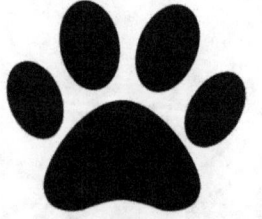

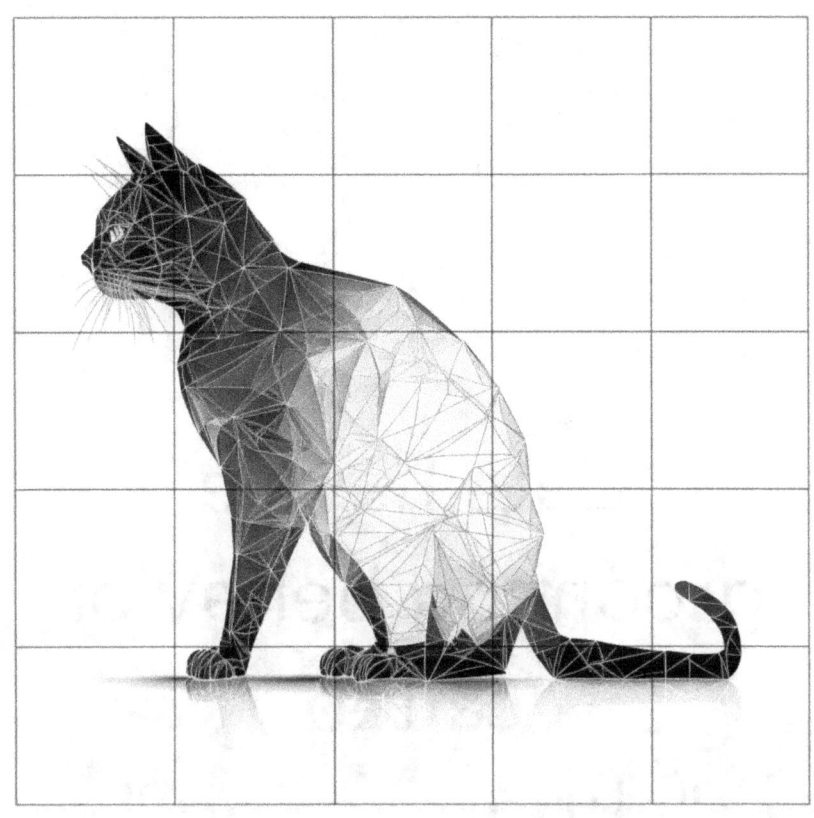

Cats have a
grooming behavior
called
"allogrooming,"
where they groom
each other to
strengthen social
bonds.

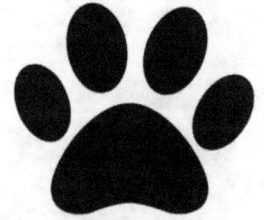

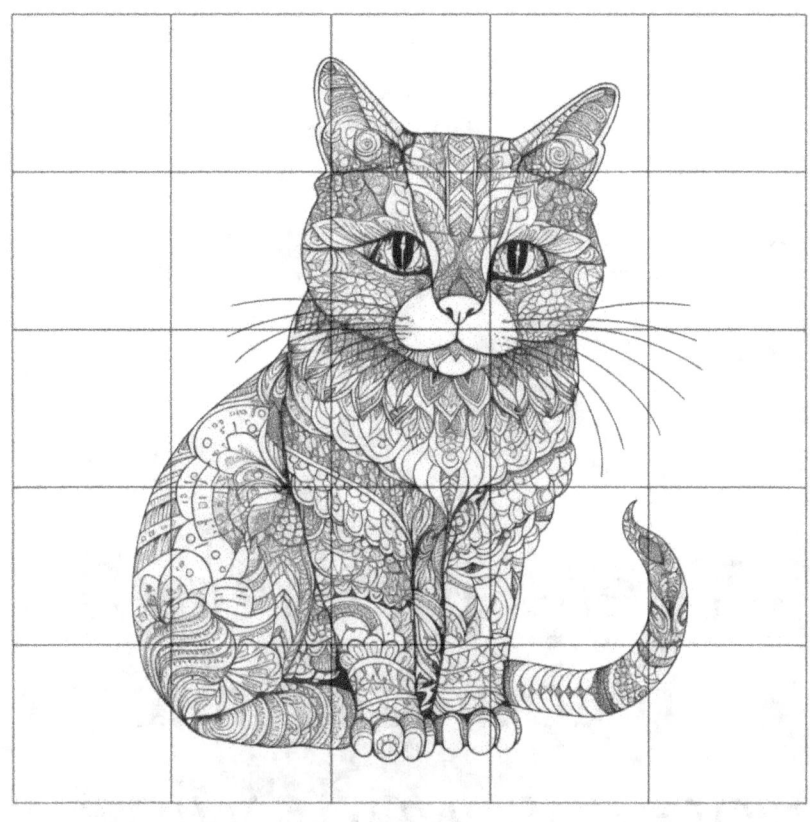

There are over 70 recognized cat breeds worldwide, with varying physical characteristics and temperaments.

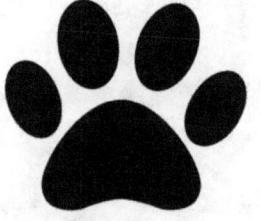

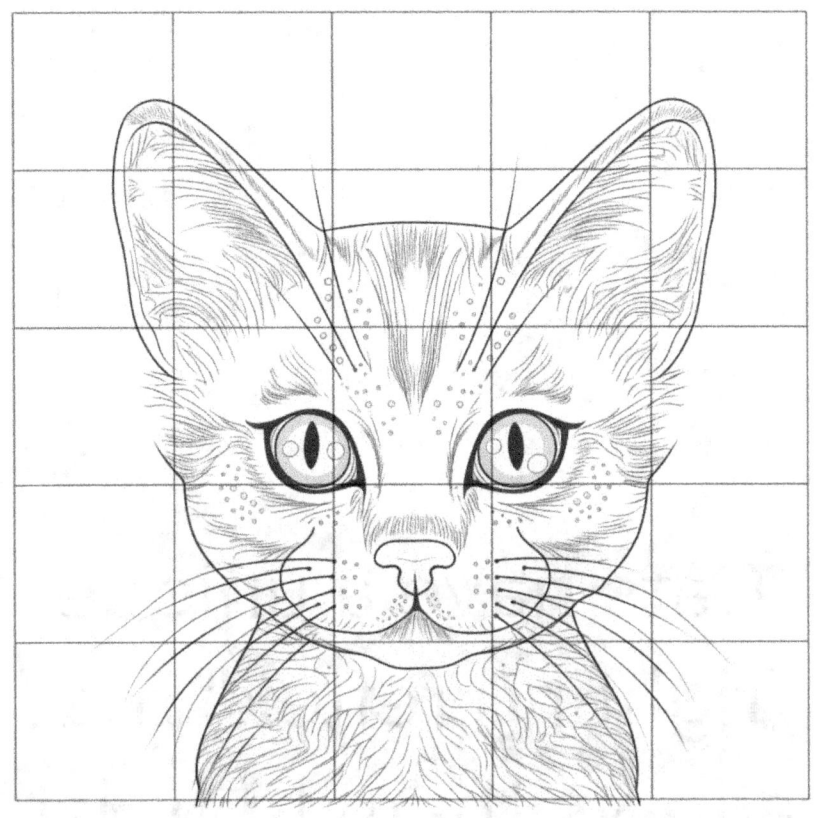

Cats have a unique "righting reflex" that allows them to twist their bodies and land on their feet when falling from heights.

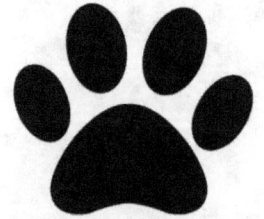

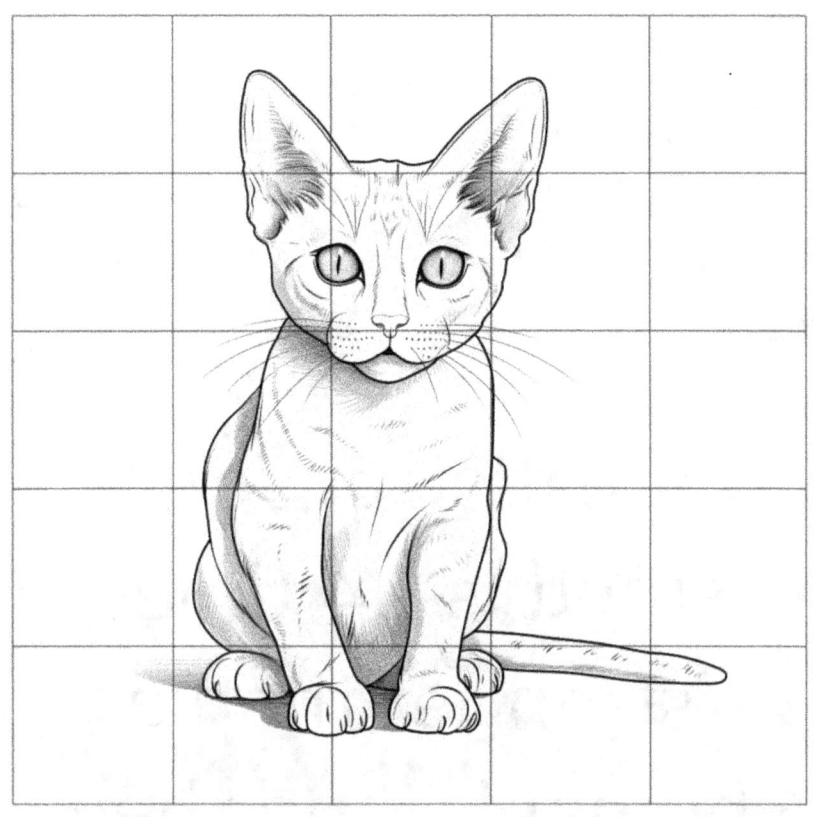

A cat's sense of smell is 14 times stronger than a human's, and they use it to identify people, other cats, and their environment.

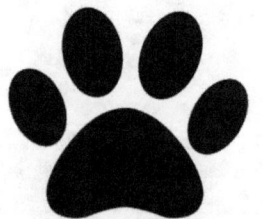

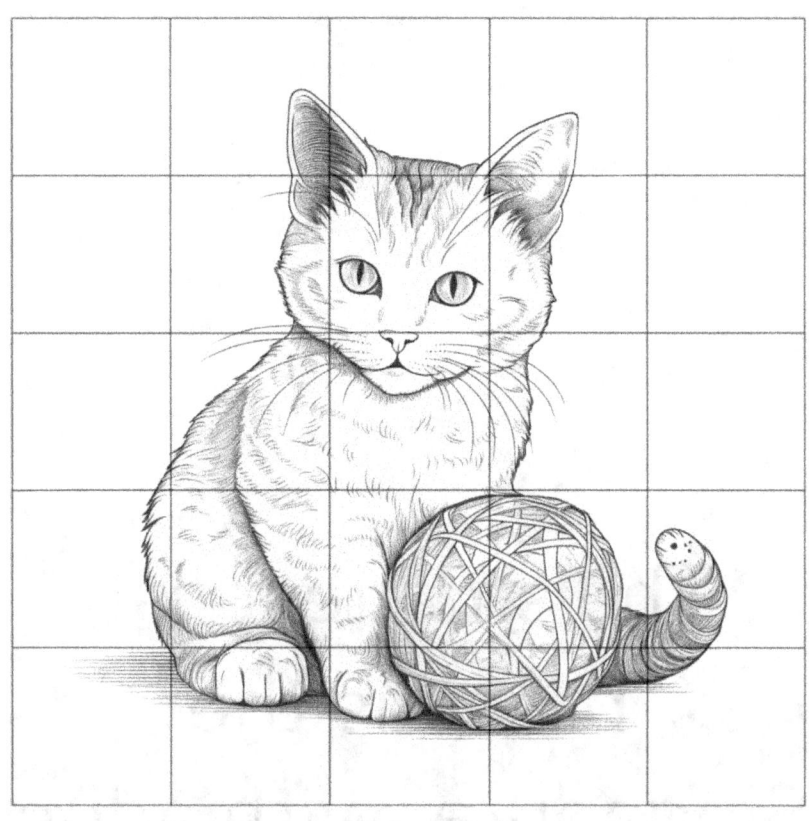

The smallest cat breed is the Singapura, with adult cats weighing between 4-8 pounds (1.8-3.6 kg).

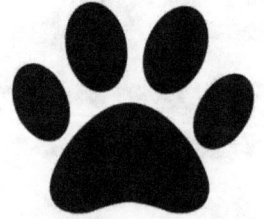

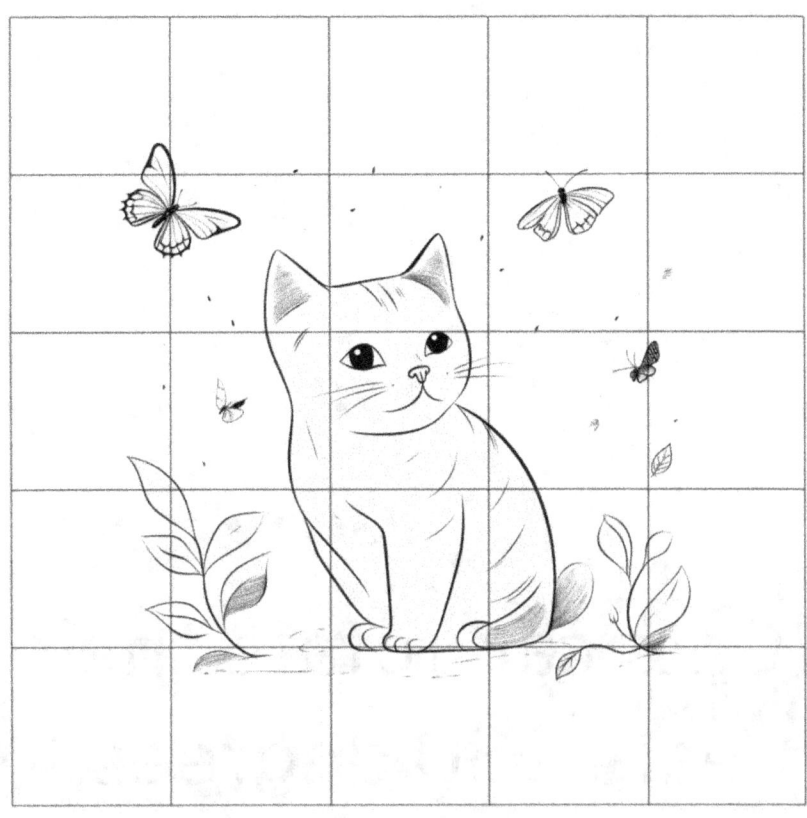

Cats can rotate their ears 180 degrees, providing them with excellent directional hearing.

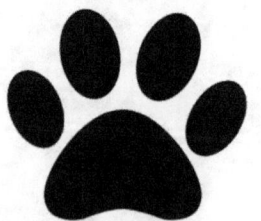

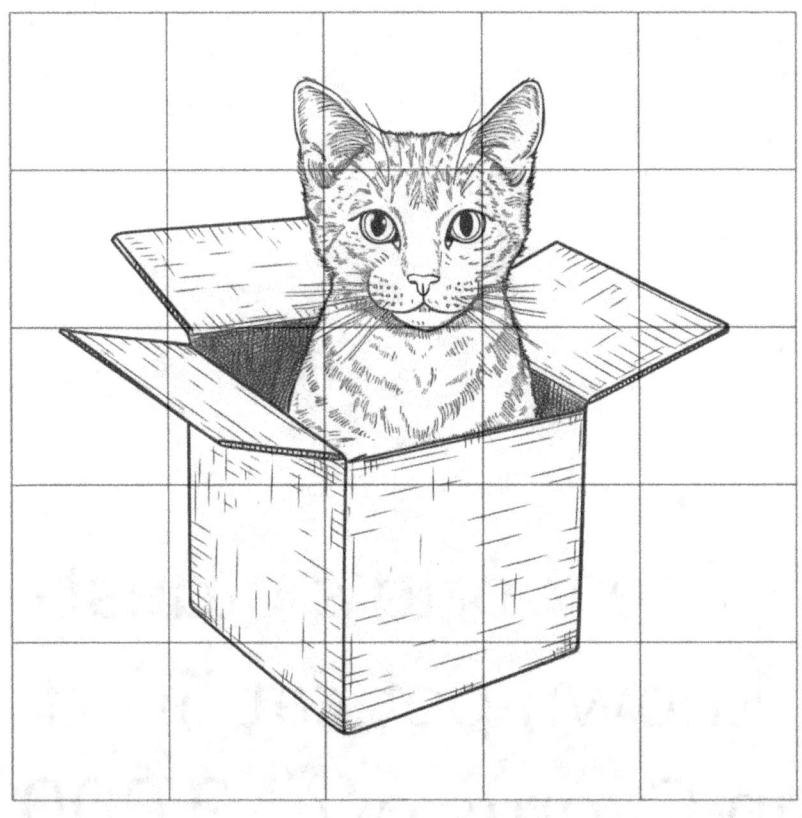

The world's oldest known pet cat lived in Cyprus over 9,000 years ago, according to an archaeological discovery.

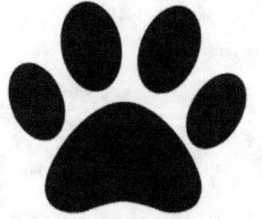

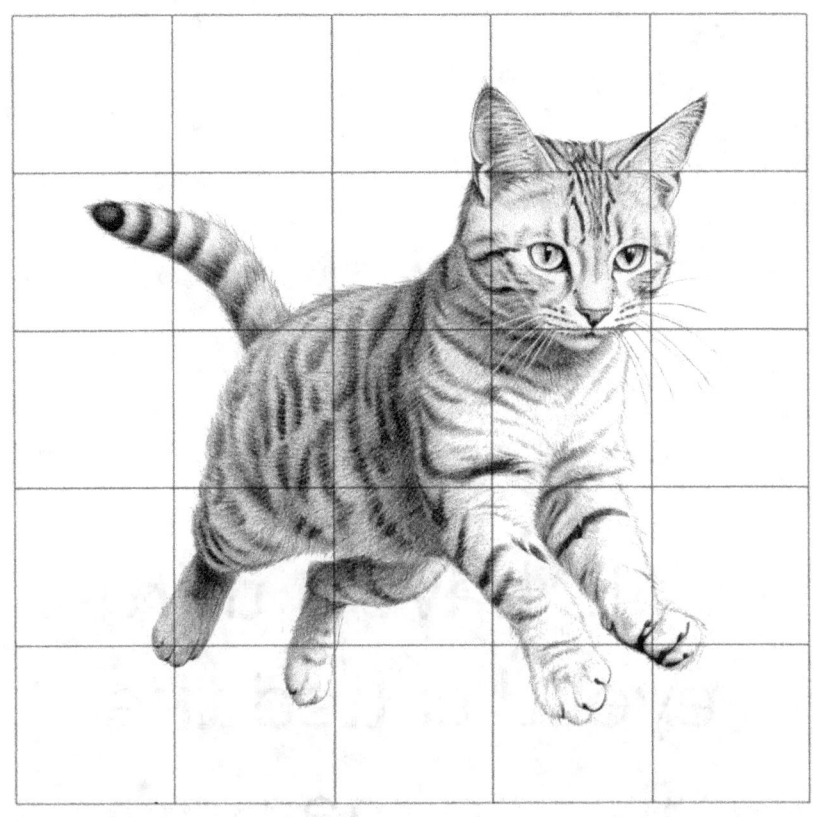

Cats have a third eyelid called the nictitating membrane that protects and moisturizes their eyes.

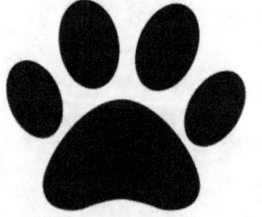

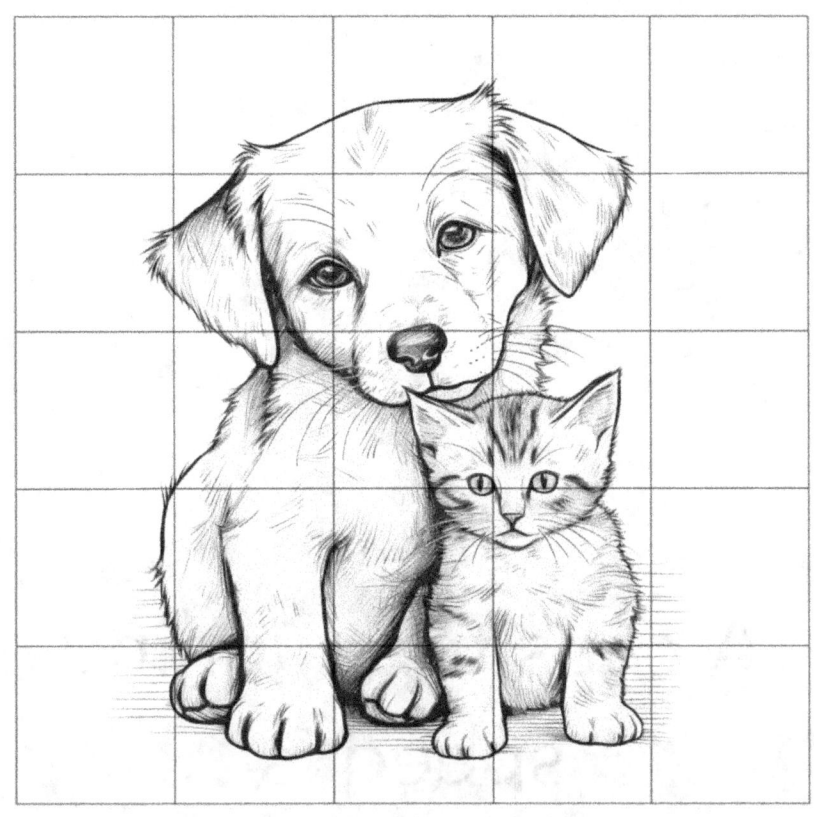

A cat's top running speed is approximately 30 mph (48 km/h) in short bursts.

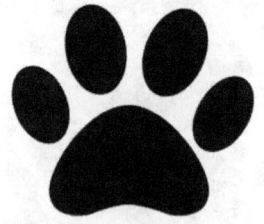

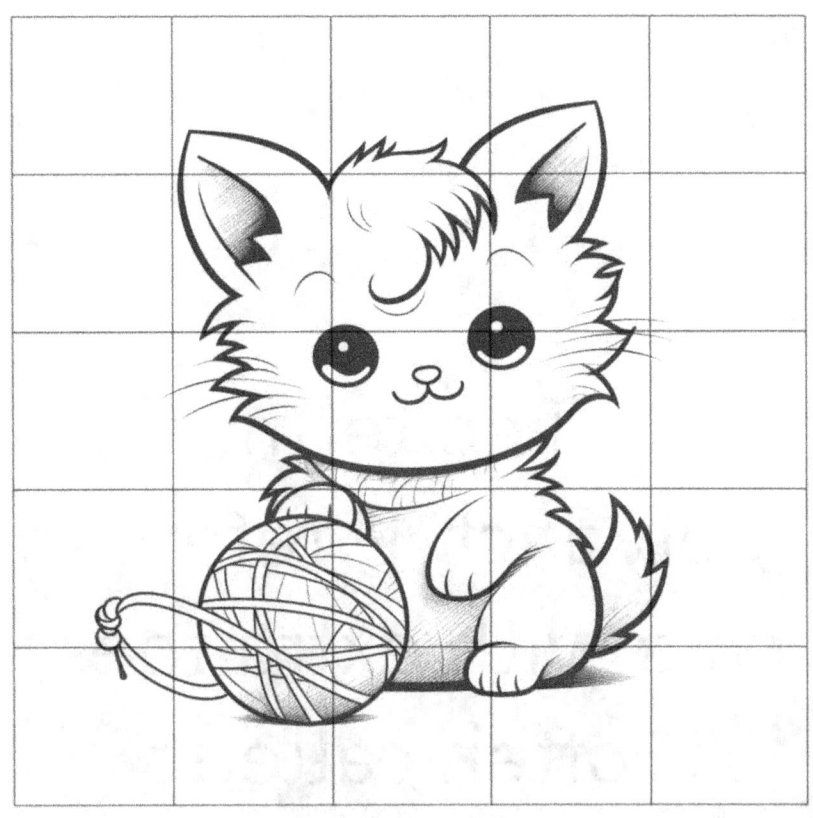

The term
"polydactyl" refers to
cats with extra toes,
often called
"Hemingway cats"
after the writer
Ernest Hemingway,
who had a fondness
for them.

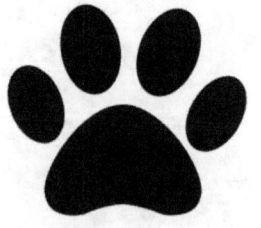

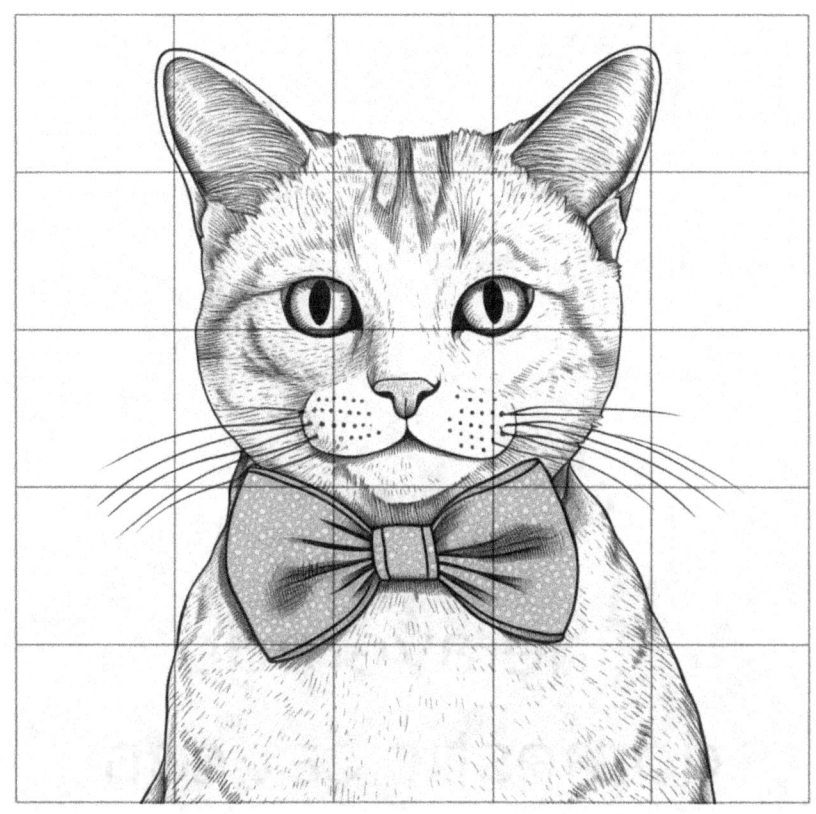

The average
domestic cat can
jump up to six times
its body length in a
single bound.

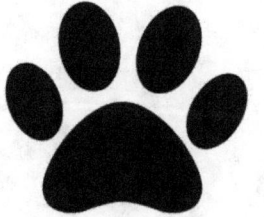

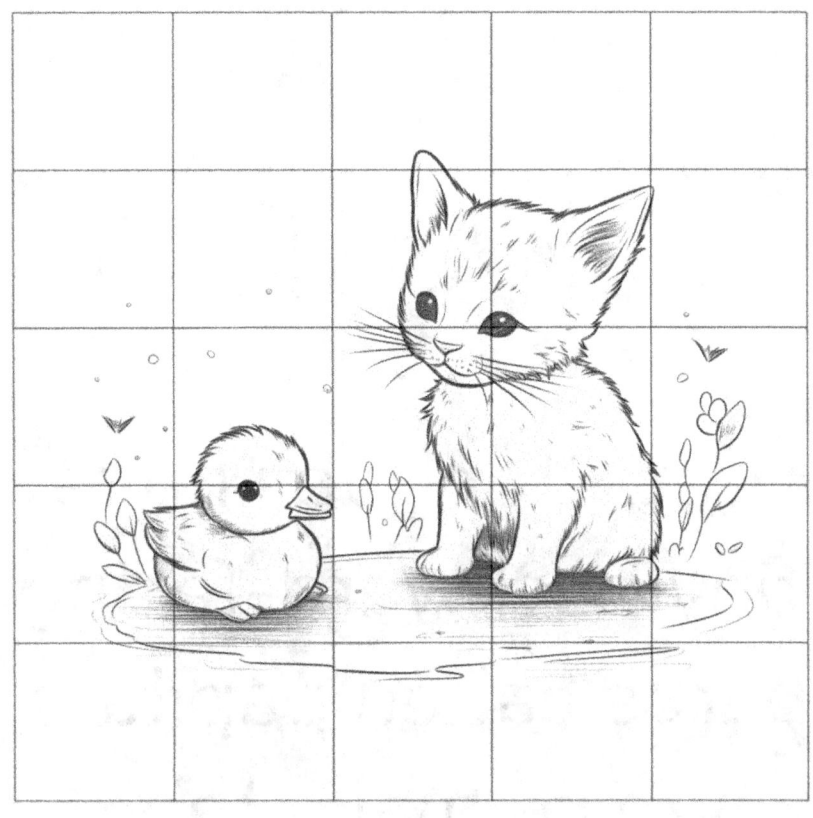

Cats' tongues have
tiny backward-facing
barbs called papillae,
which make their
tongues rough and
efficient for grooming
and lapping up
water.

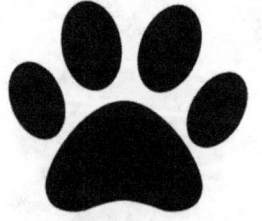

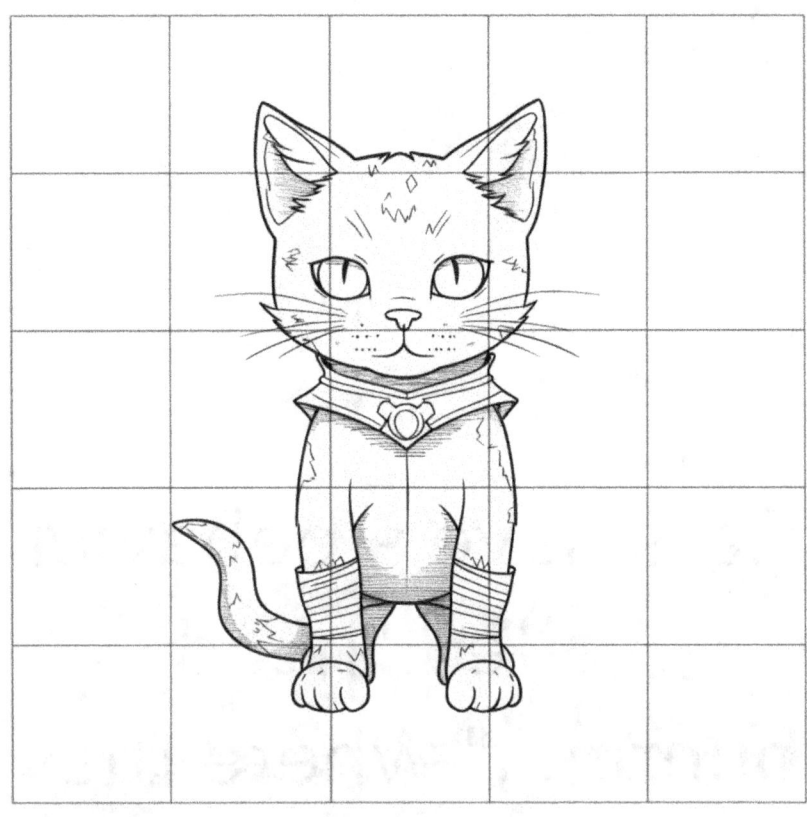

Cats have a behavior called "head bunting," where they bump their heads against a person or object as a sign of affection.

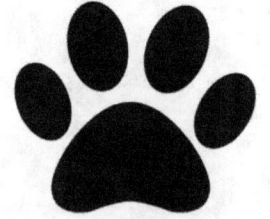

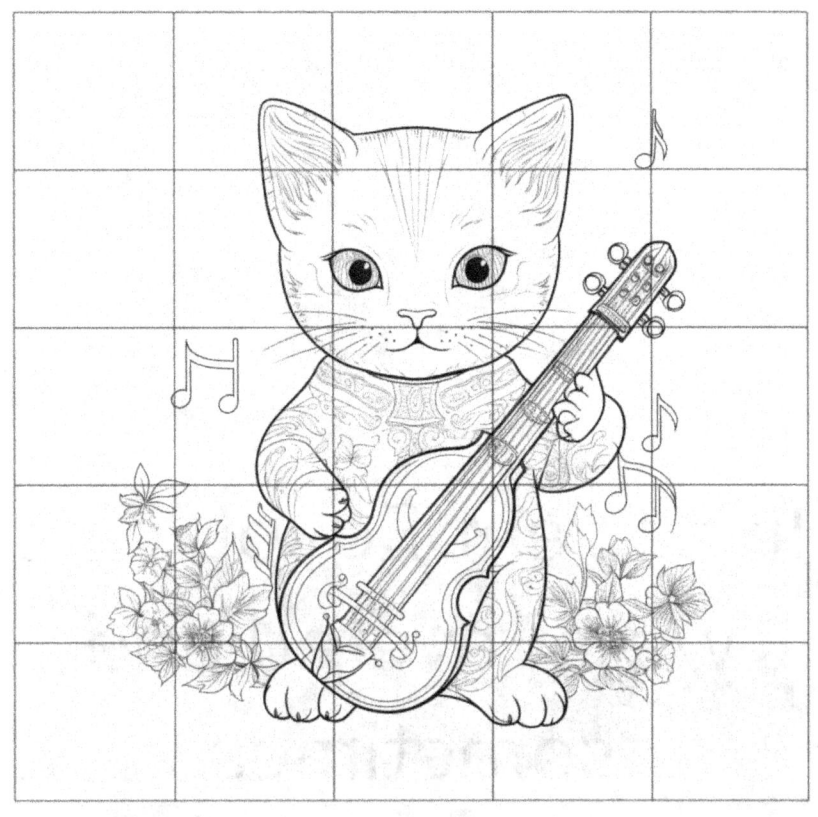

In ancient Egypt, cats were revered and sometimes worshipped, as they were believed to possess protective qualities.

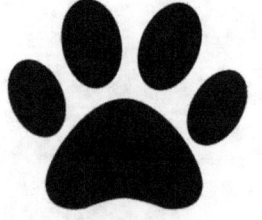

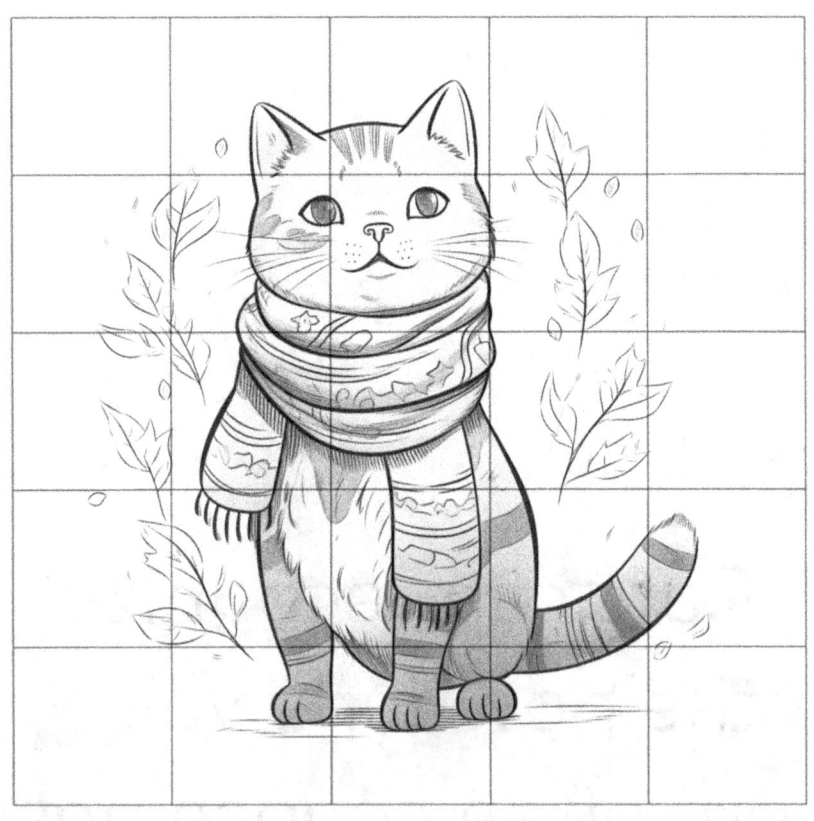

Cats can recognize
their owner's voice
but often choose not
to respond,
demonstrating their
independent nature.

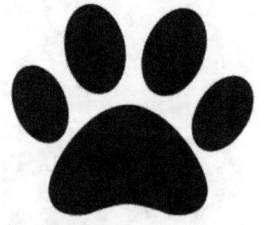

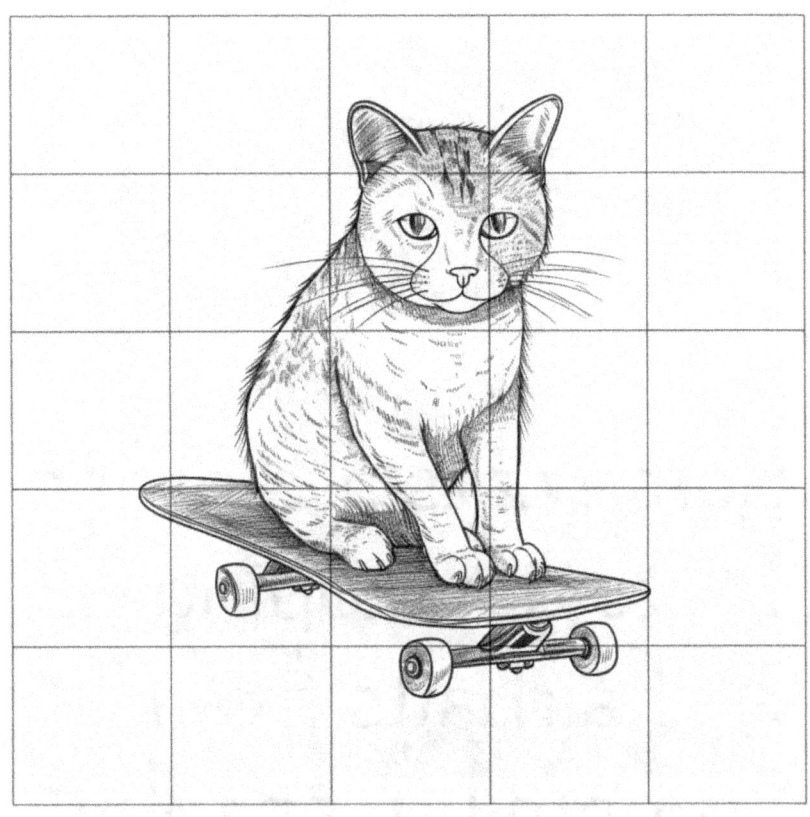

Some cats are prone to developing hairballs from grooming, as they swallow loose hair that then accumulates in their stomach.

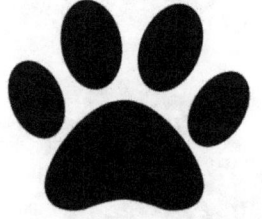

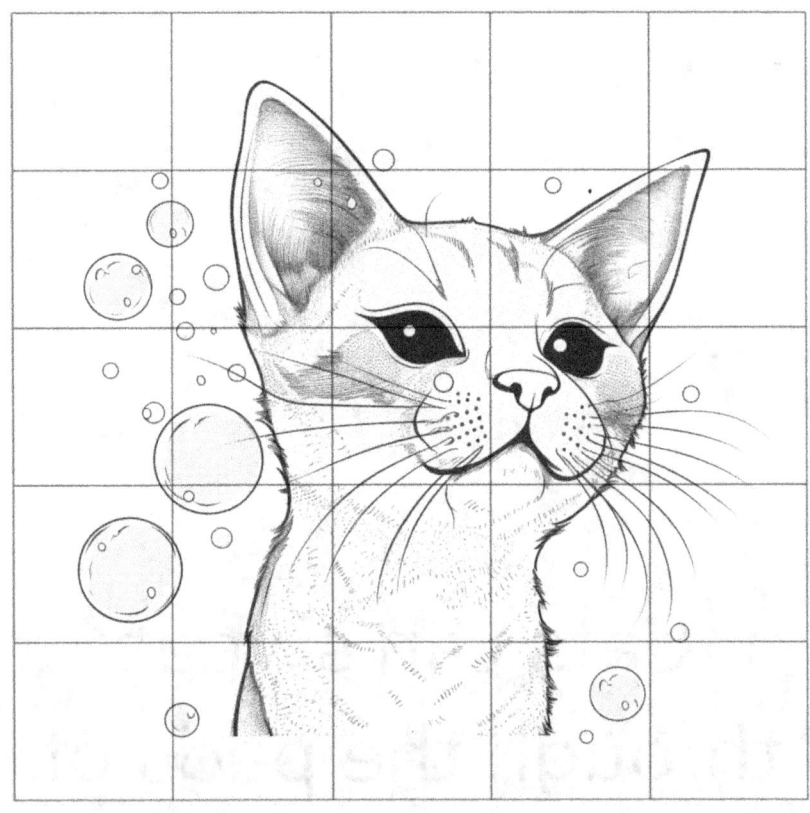

Cats can sweat
through the pads of
their paws to help
regulate their body
temperature.

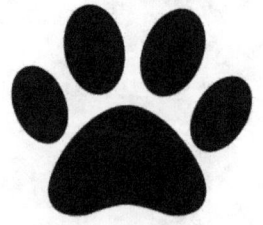

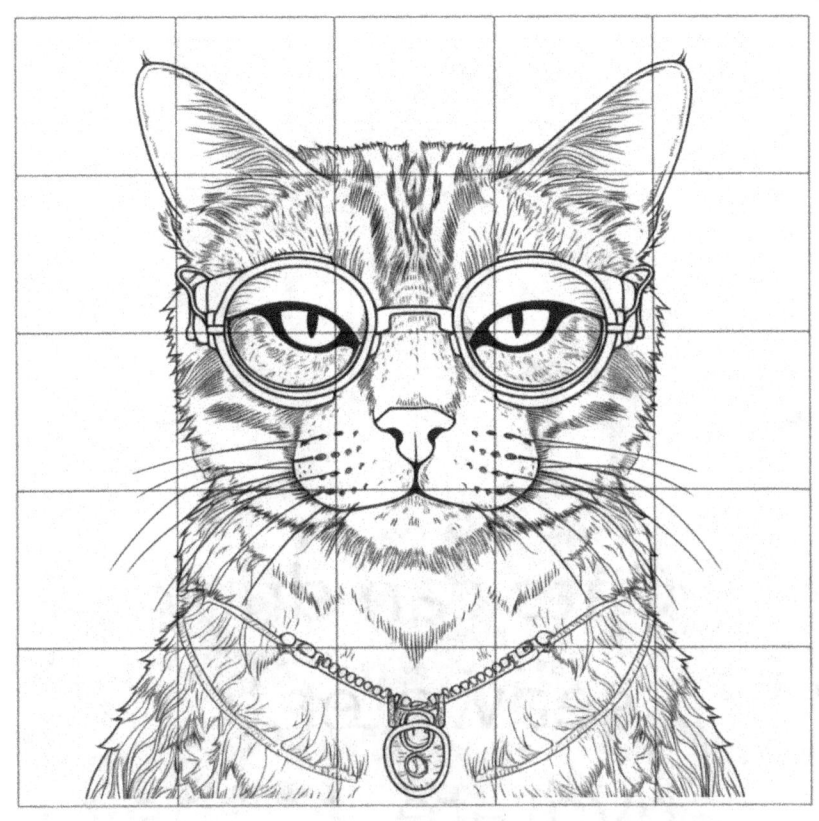

Cats can drink
seawater to
rehydrate, as their
kidneys can
efficiently filter out
the salt.

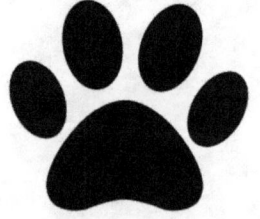

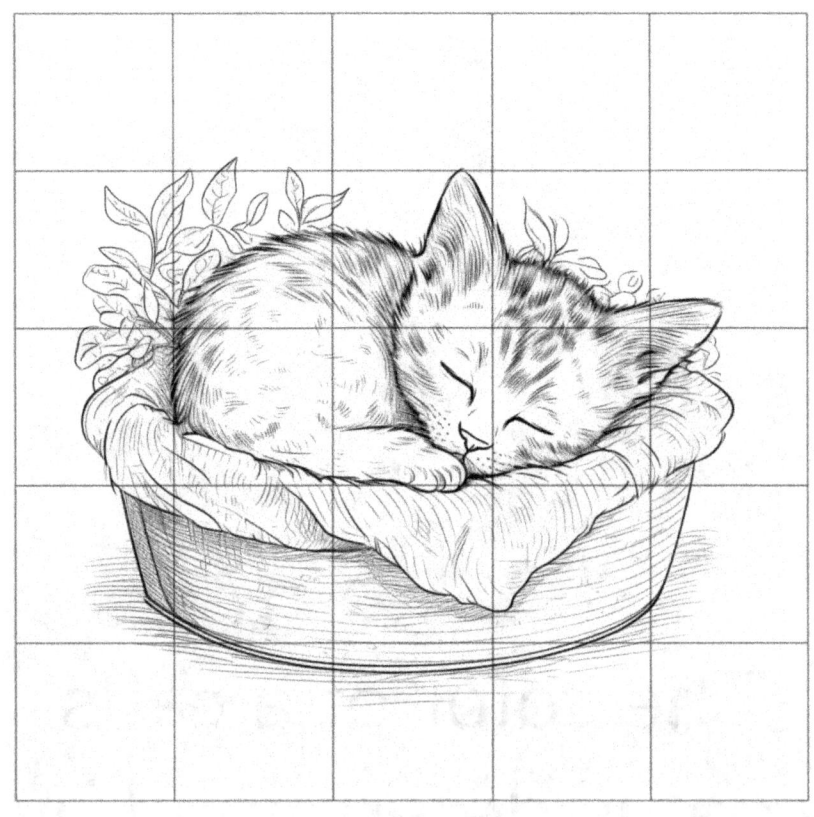

The color of a cat's coat is determined by various genes that control pigmentation.

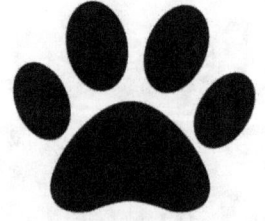

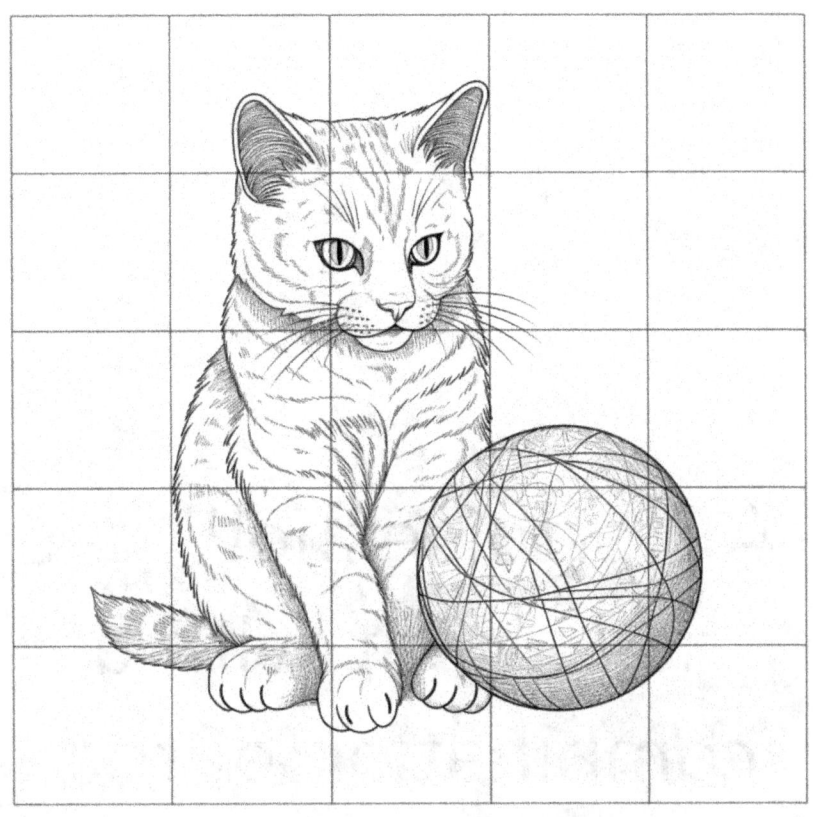

A "tortoiseshell" cat has a coat with a combination of red and black fur, while a "calico" cat has a coat with red, black, and white fur.

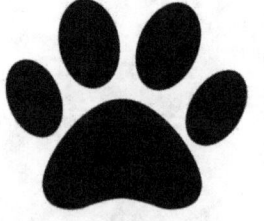

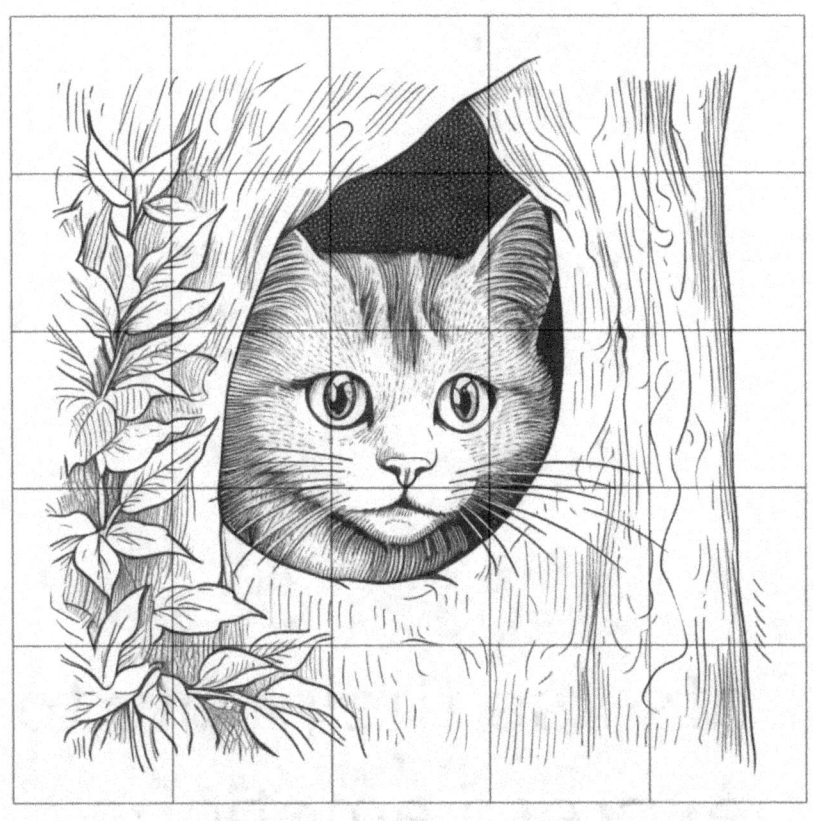

Cats use their tails to
express emotions,
such as happiness,
fear, or aggression.

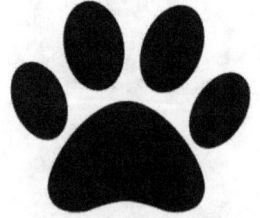

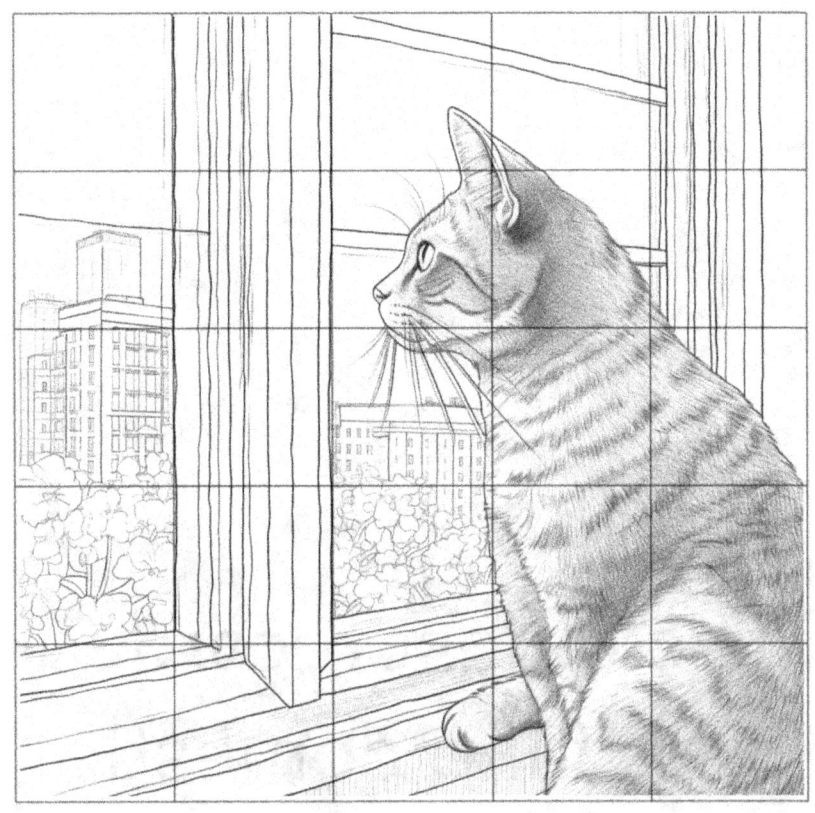

The oldest recorded
age for a domestic
cat was 38 years,
held by a cat named
Creme Puff.

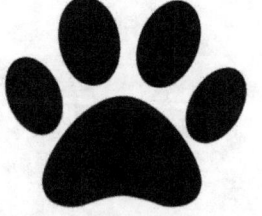

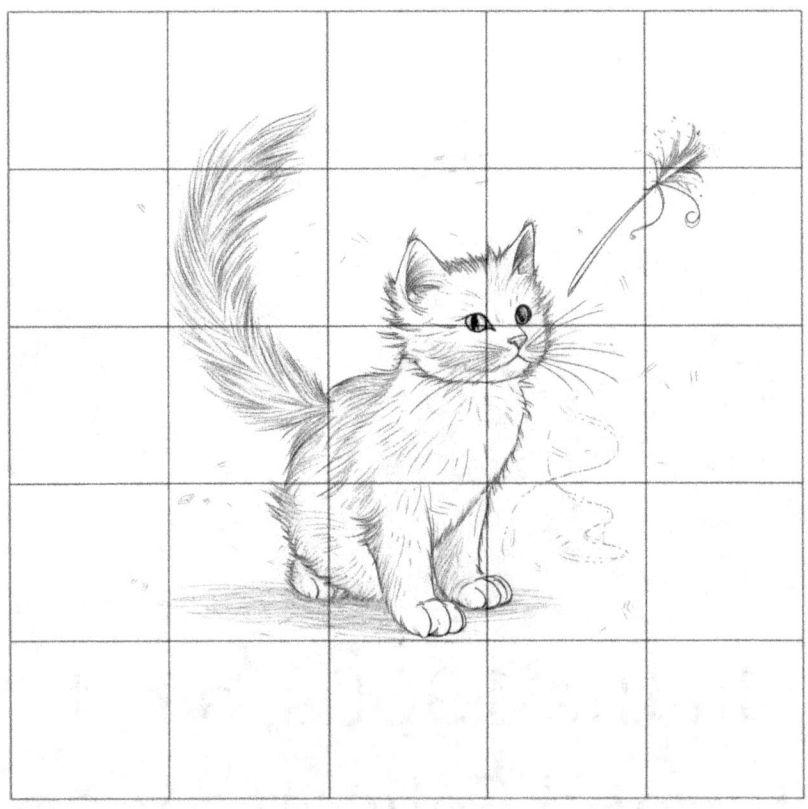

In the 1960s, a cat named Félicette was the first and only cat to travel to space.

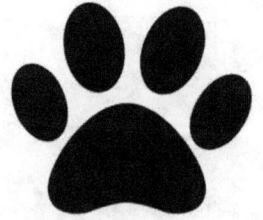

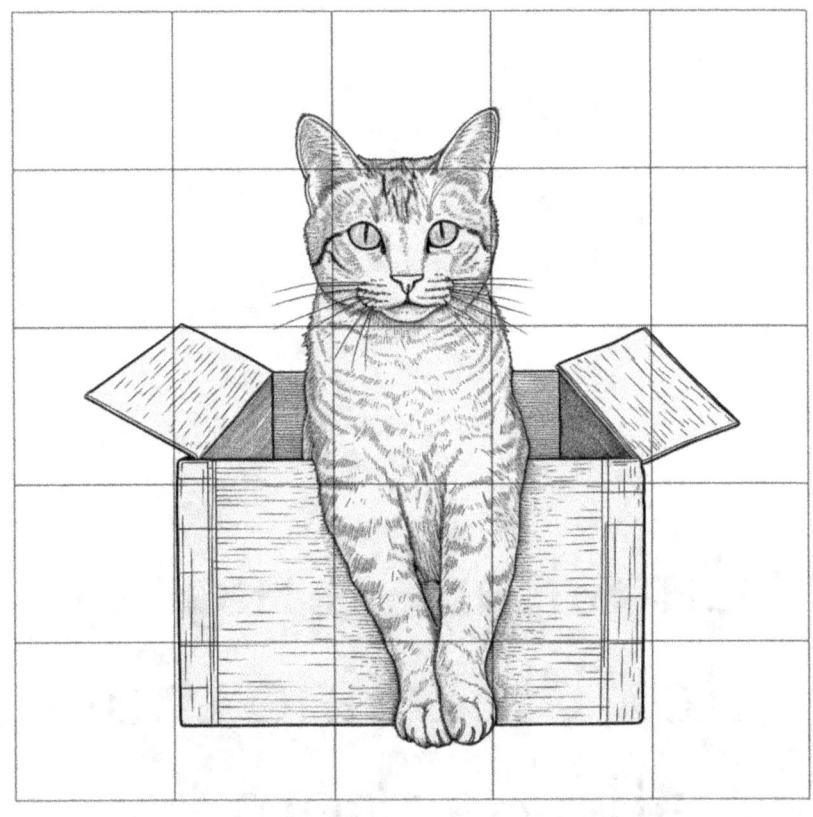

Cats have a highly flexible spine that allows them to contort their bodies and fit through tight spaces.

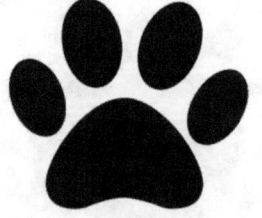

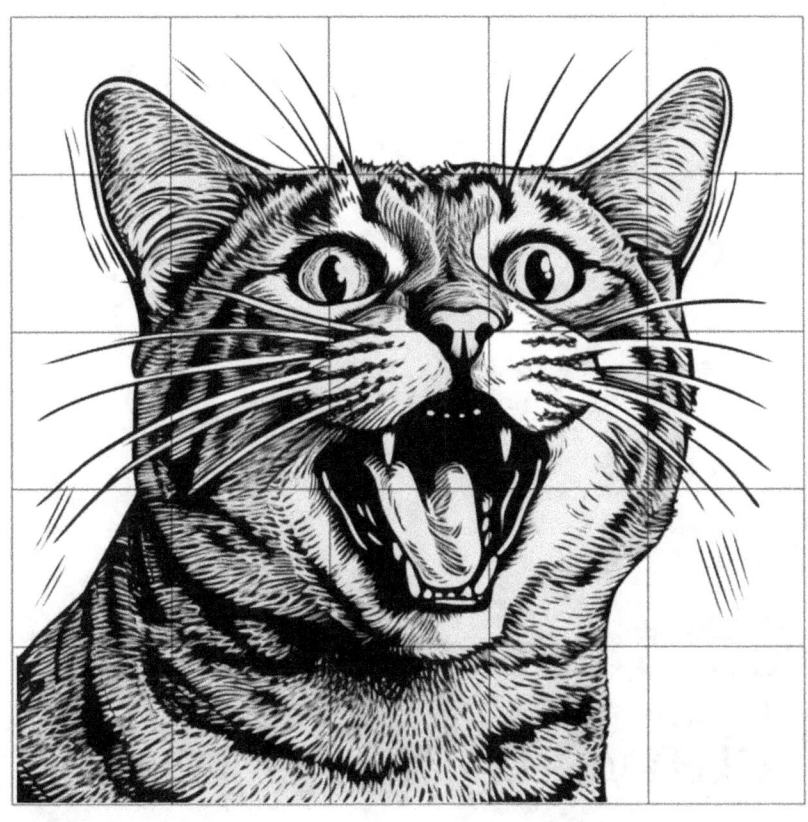

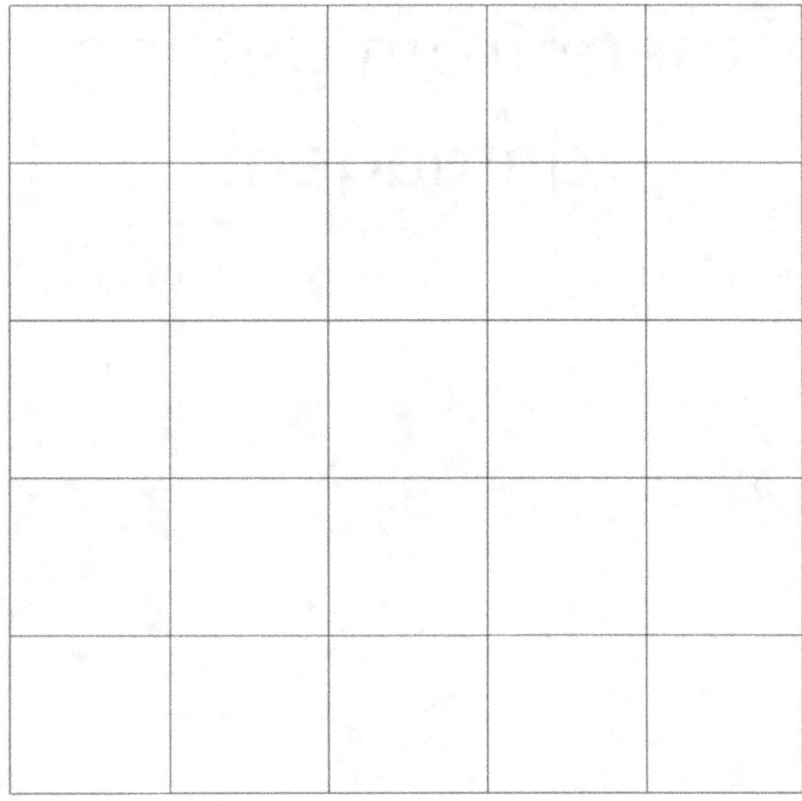

Cats can retract their claws to keep them sharp and prevent them from getting damaged.

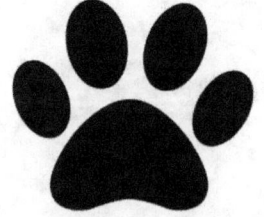

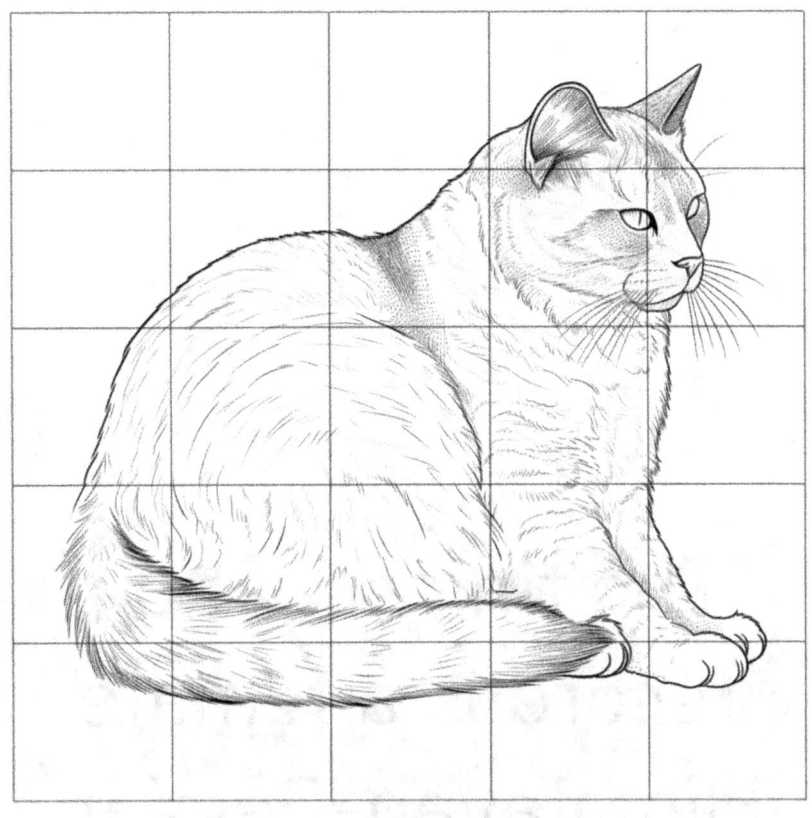

The tiniest cat on record is a female Himalayan-Persian named Tinker Toy, who stood only 2.75 inches tall.

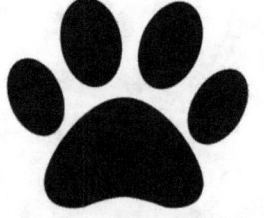

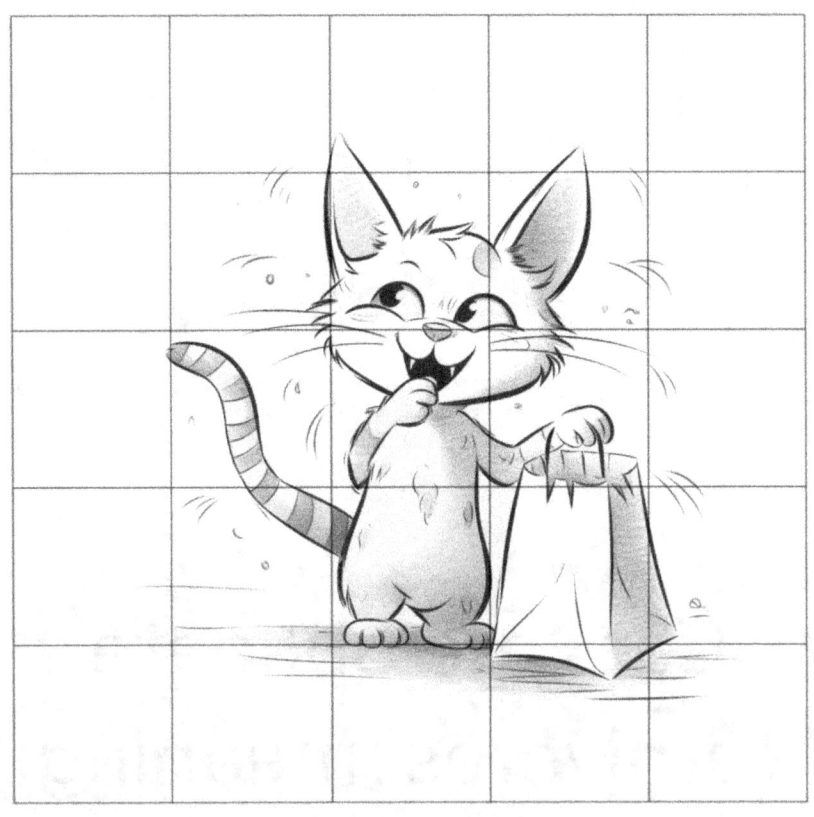

Cats are obligate
carnivores, meaning
they require a diet
that consists mainly
of meat to survive.

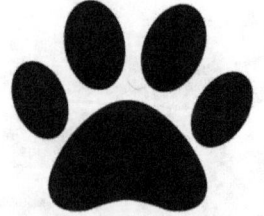

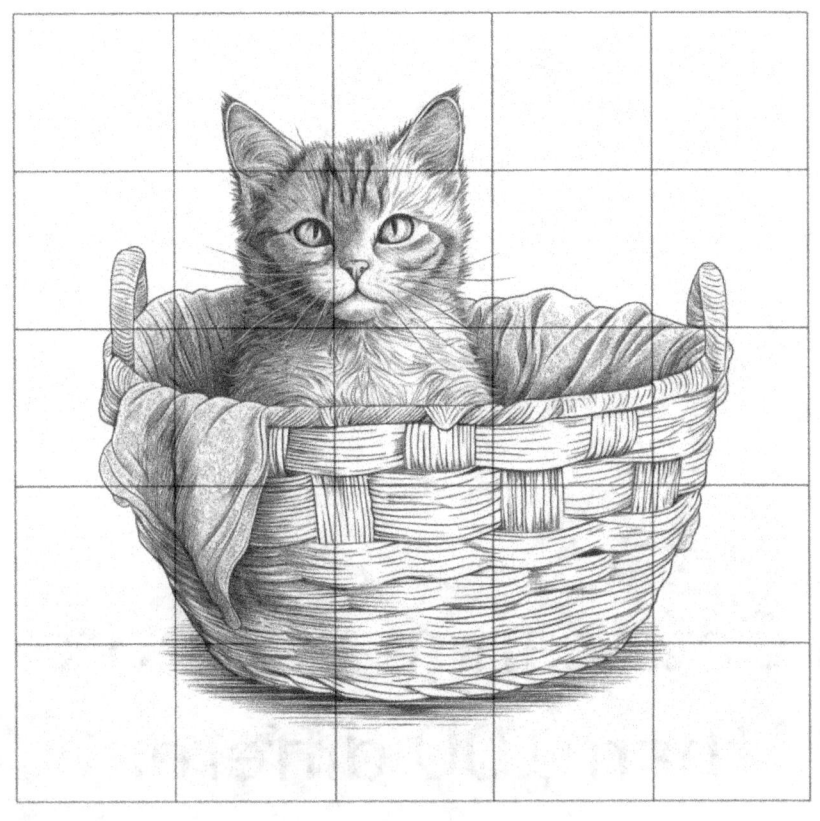

Cats can make more than 100 different sounds, including meows, purrs, hisses, and chirps.

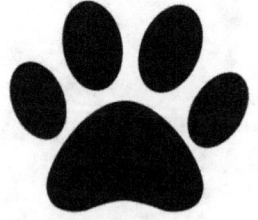

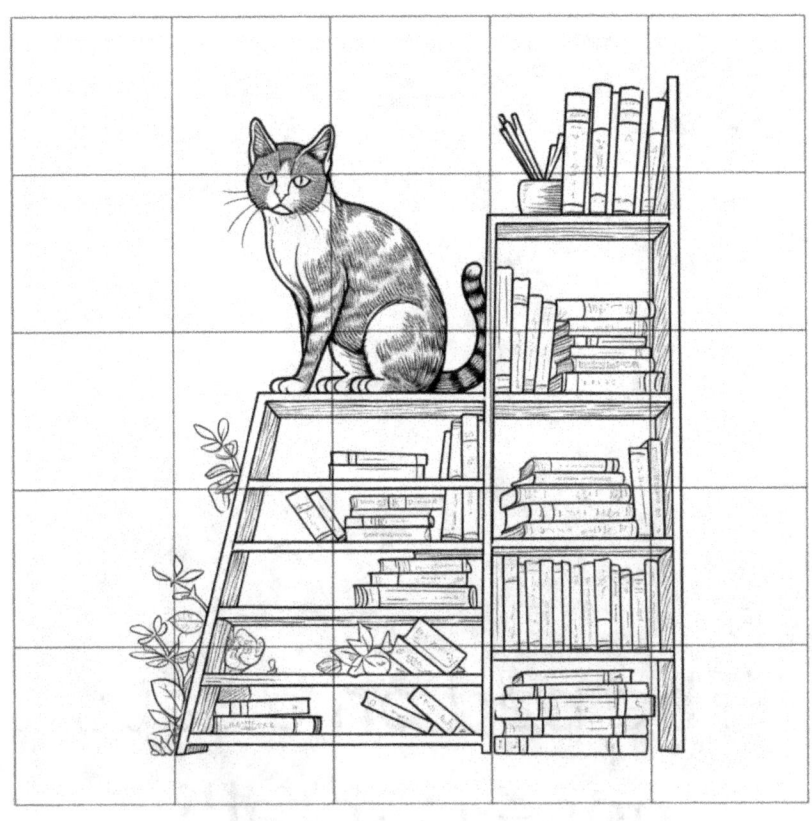

The pad on a cat's nose is totally unique, a lot like a person's fingerprint.

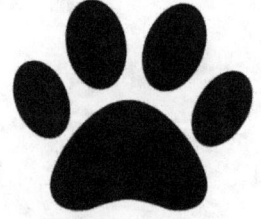

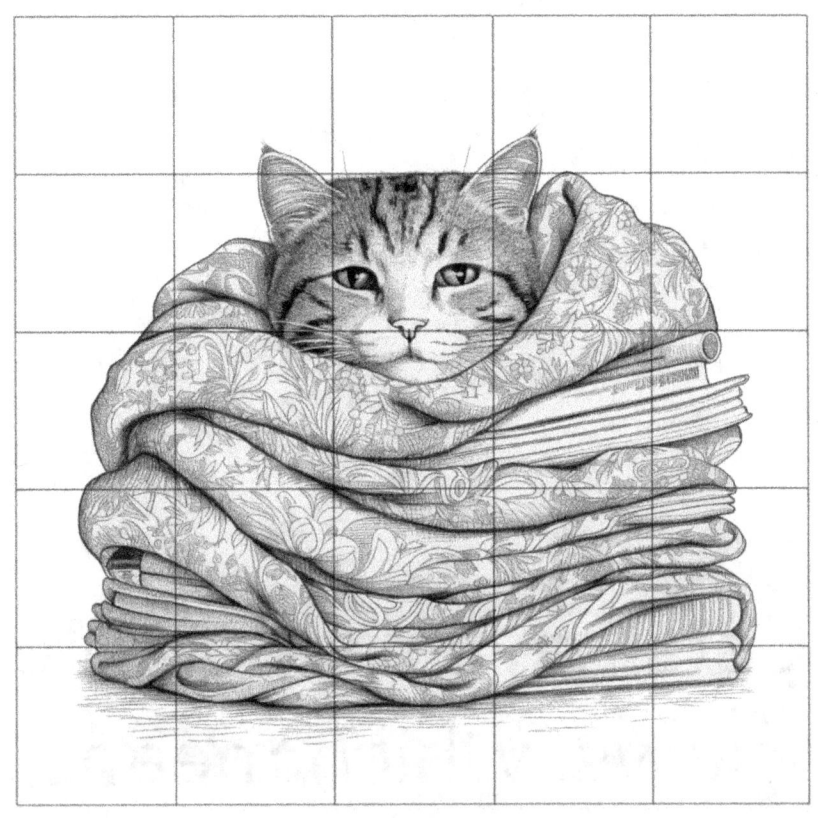

Cats have retractable claws, which means that the claws are sheathed when not in use.

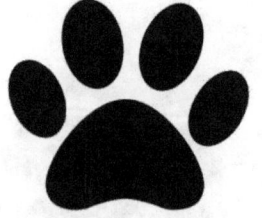

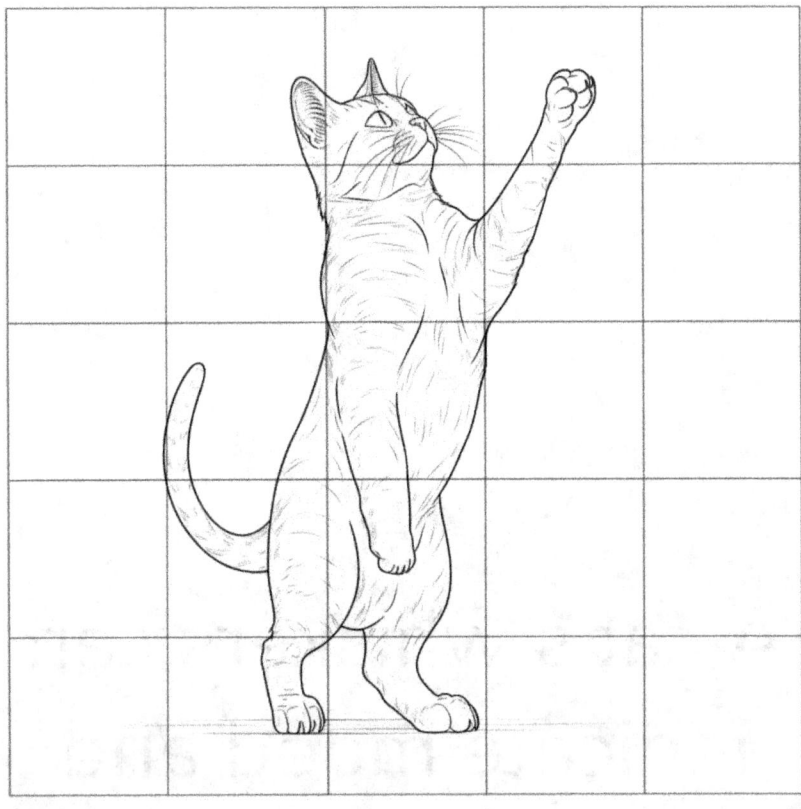

A cat's whiskers can indicate mood and help them judge distances.

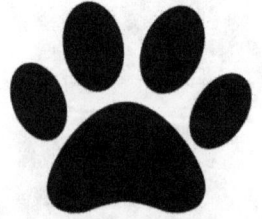

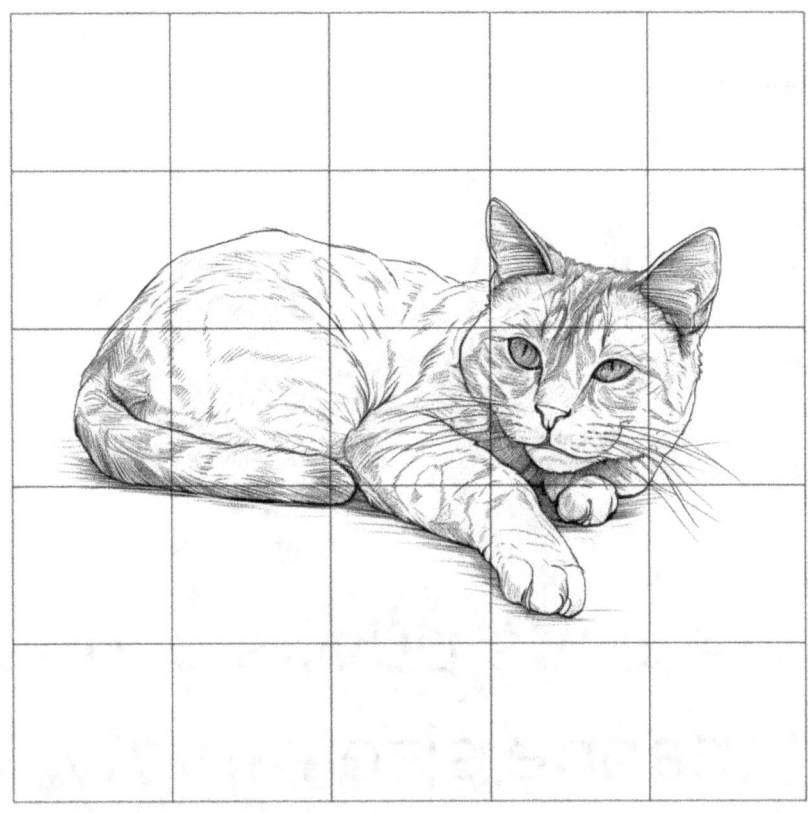

A cat's pupils can
change size rapidly,
allowing them to
adjust to different
levels of light.

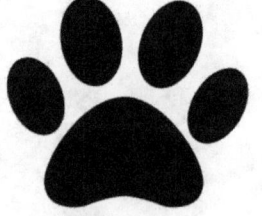

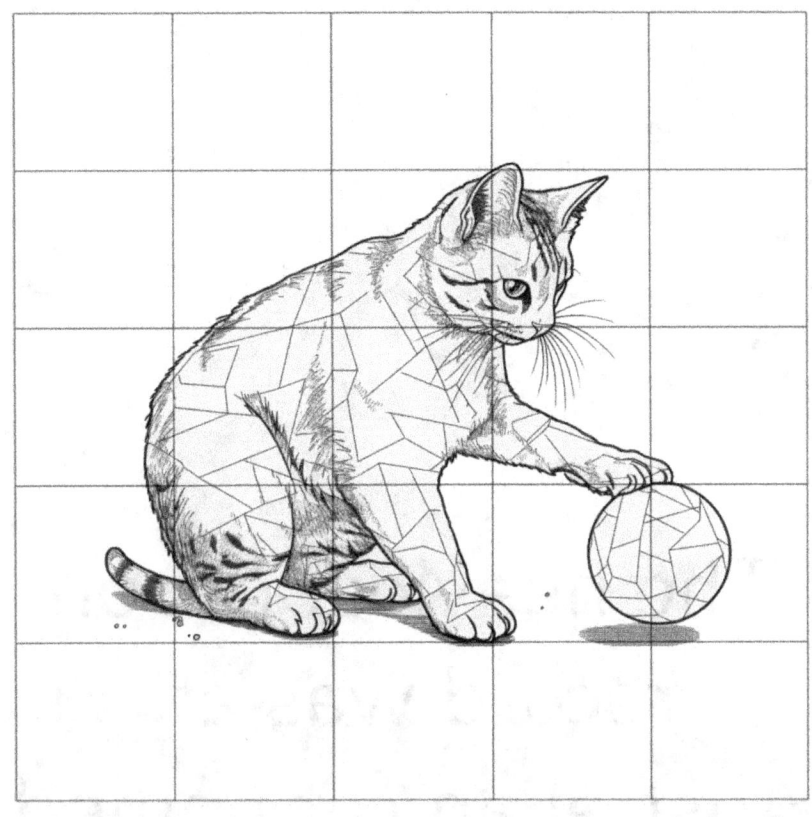

The heaviest cat on record was an Australian cat named Himmy, who weighed over 46 pounds.

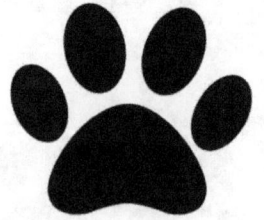

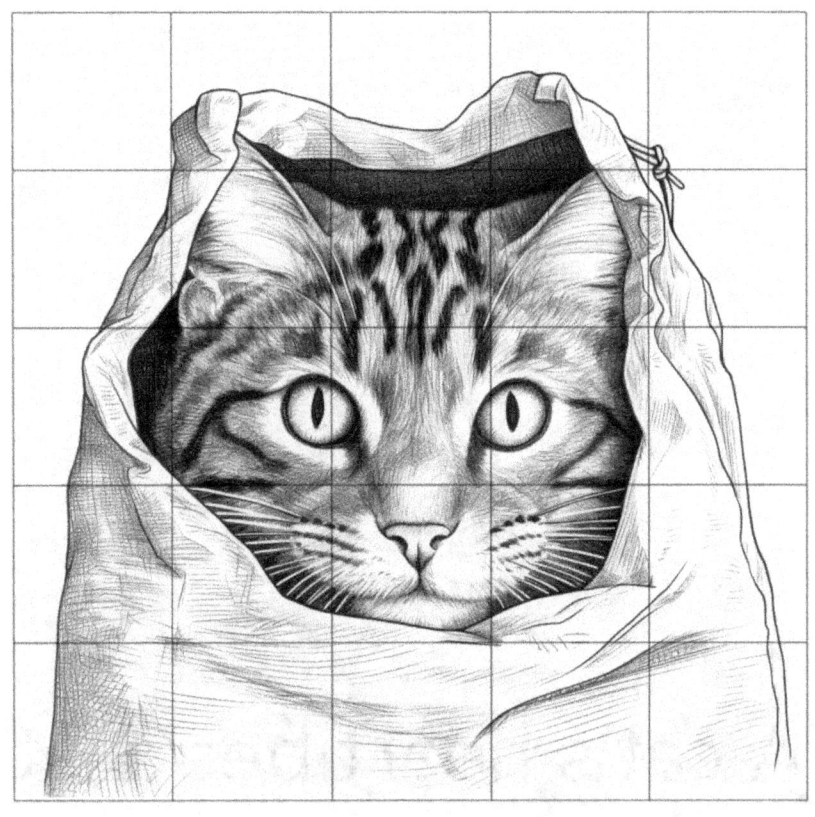

A cat's heart beats at a rate of 120-140 beats per minute.

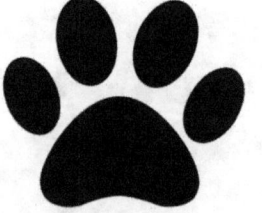

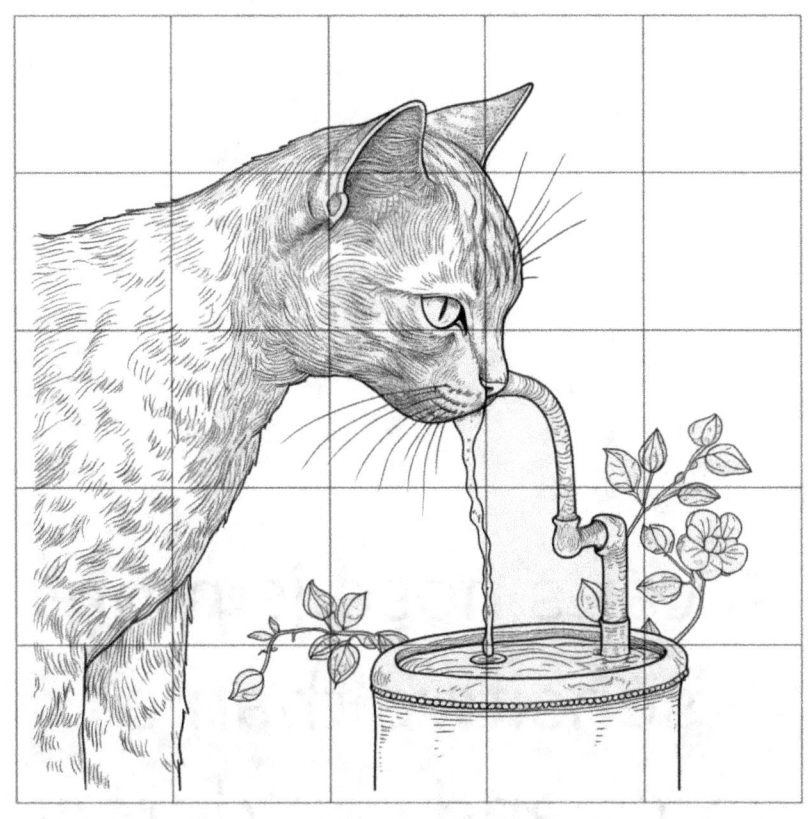
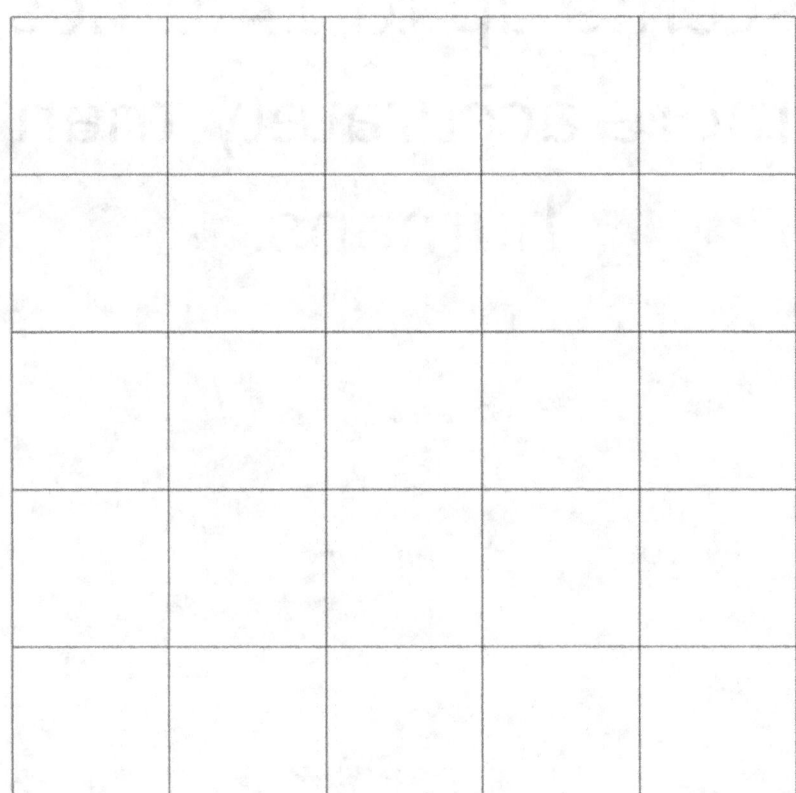

A cat's nose is more
sensitive than a
dog's and can detect
scents up to 14 times
more accurately than
humans.

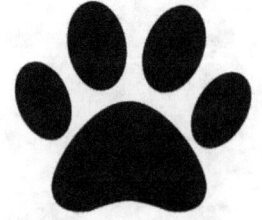

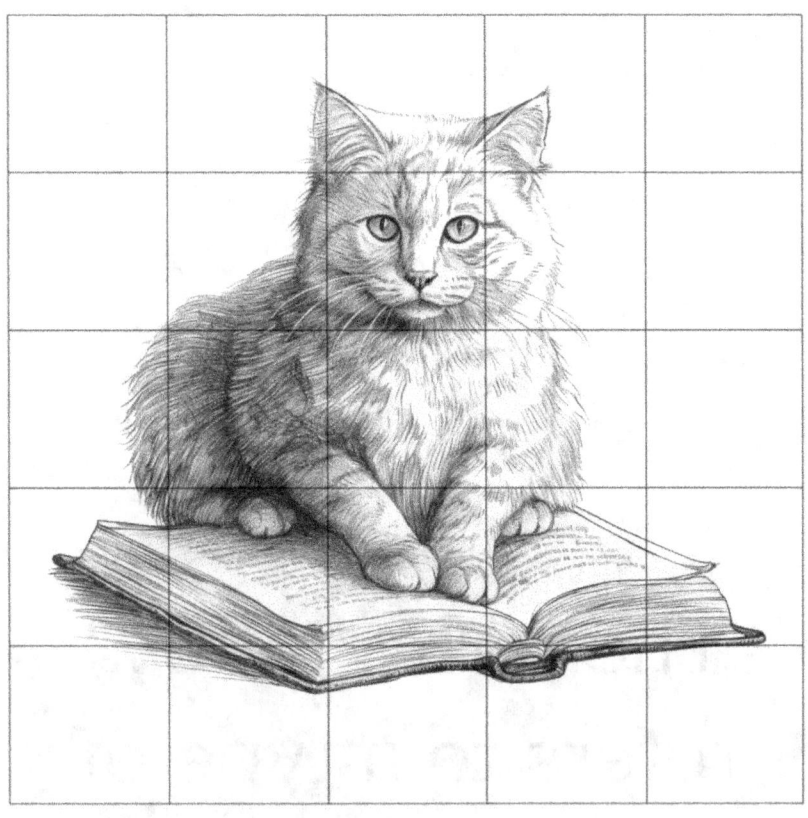

The term "tabby" refers to a type of coat pattern that features stripes, dots, or swirling patterns.

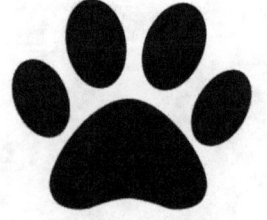

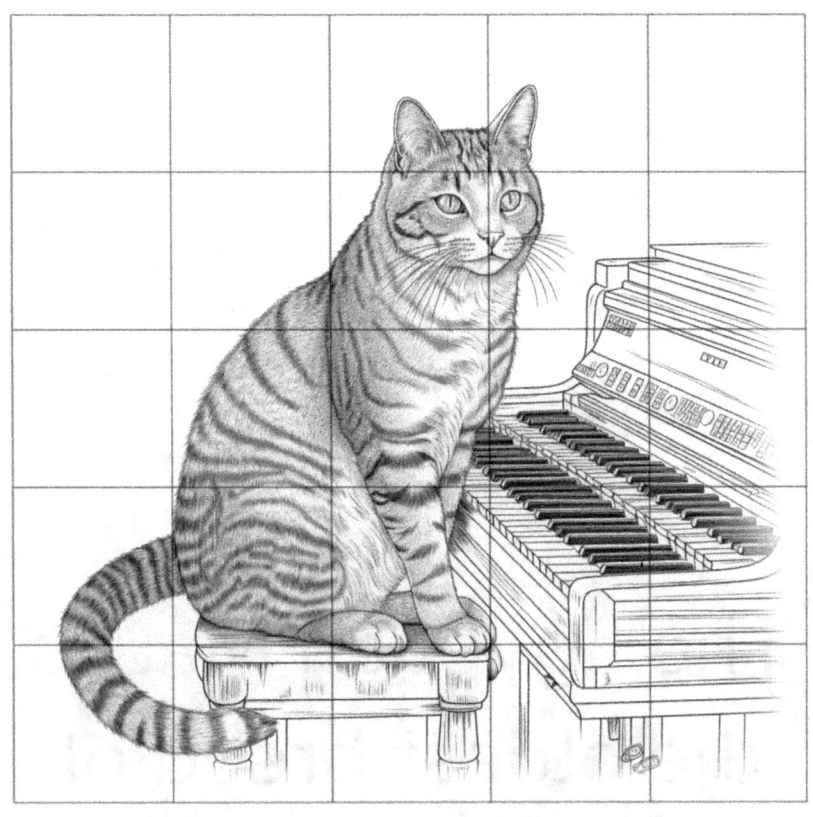

The Egyptian Mau is the oldest breed of domestic cat, dating back to ancient Egypt.

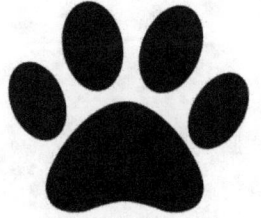

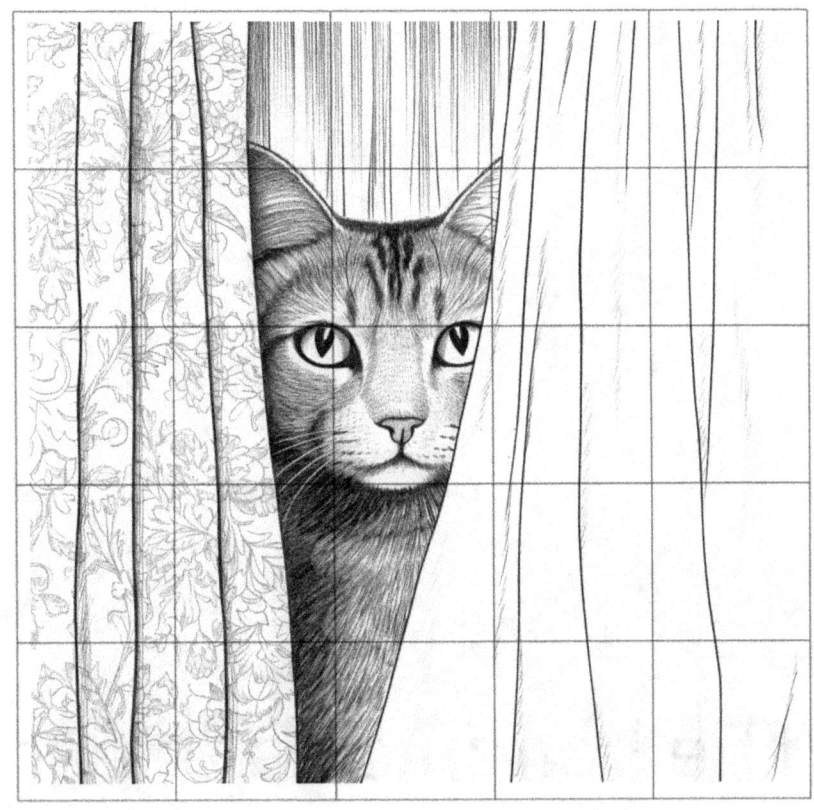

The hair in a cat's ear
is called ear
furnishings.

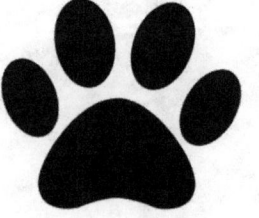

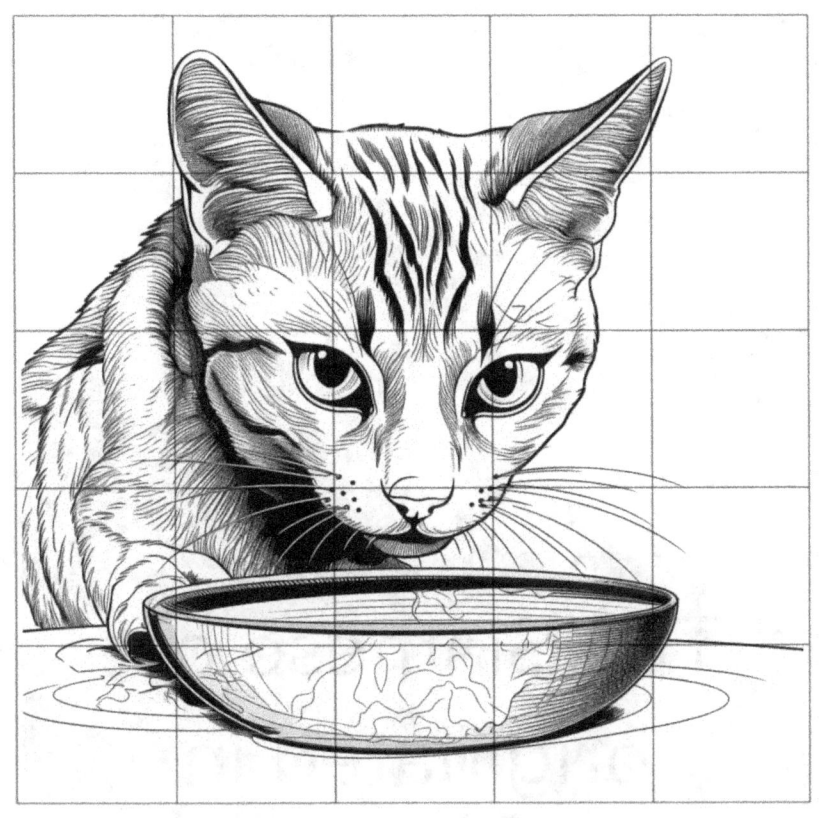

The Siamese cat
originated in
Thailand and was
once considered
sacred.

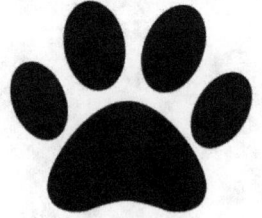

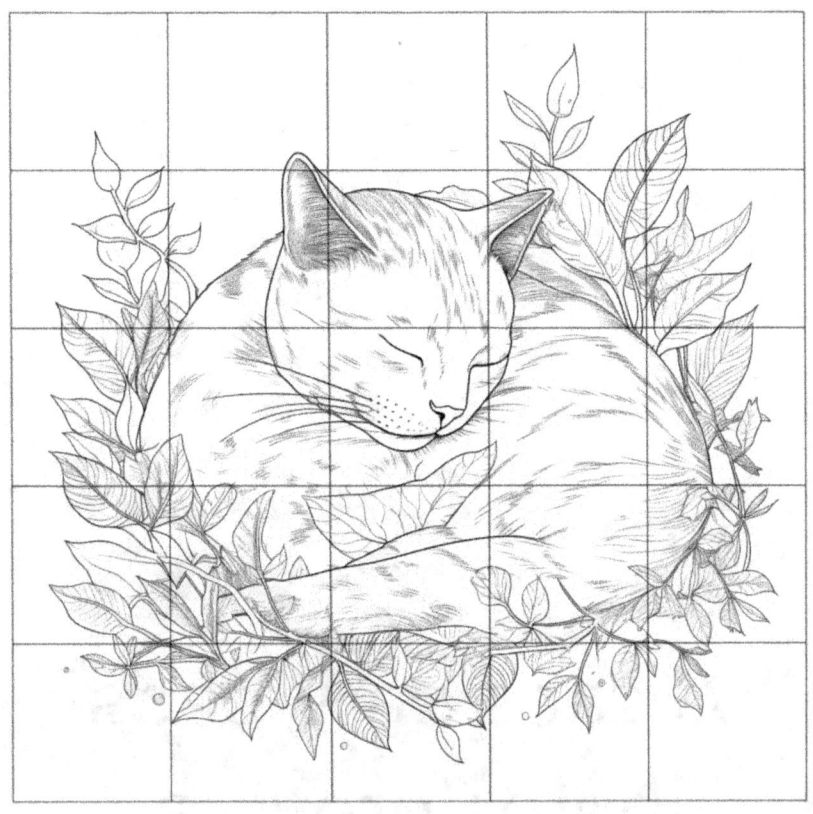

A cat's paw pads
helps provide
traction and act as
shock absorbers.

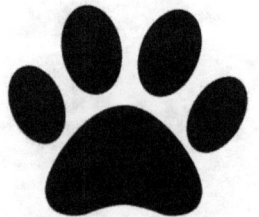

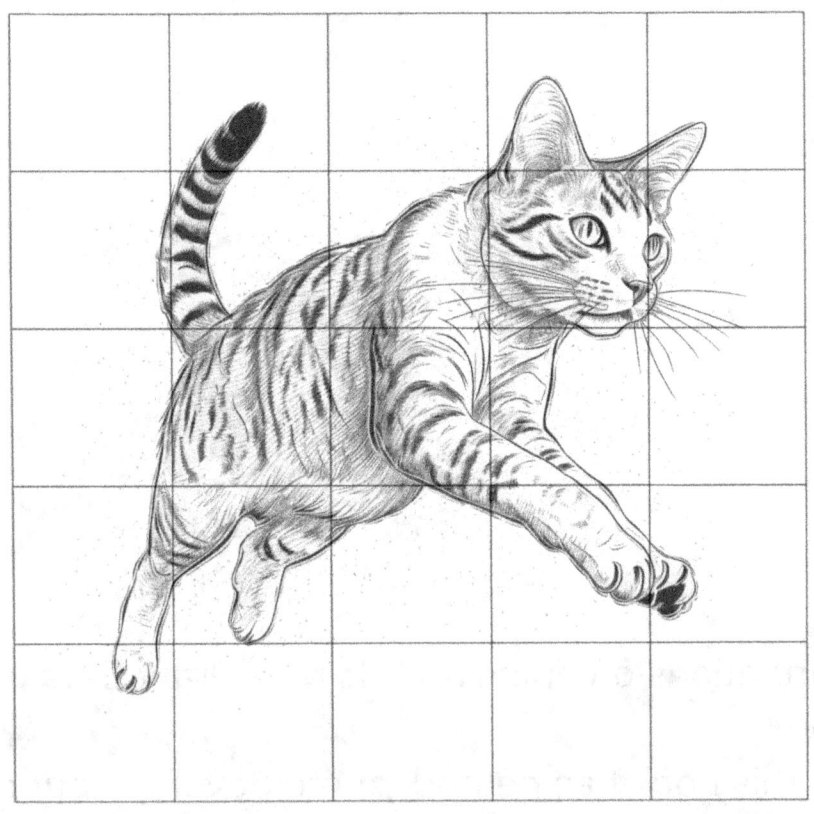

Congratulations on finishing "How to Draw Cats by Grid"

We hope that this book has helped you to develop your drawing skills and provided you with many hours of creative enjoyment.

We want to thank you again for choosing our book and hope that you will continue to enjoy drawing cats and exploring your creativity. Keep up the great work, and congratulations on a job well done!